the get outside fun and learn
project and
nature book

de fun and learn

ct and
e book

**1000 brilliant step-by-step colour
pictures show you what to do when**

clare bradley and cecilia fitzsimons

southwater

This edition is published by Southwater

Southwater is an imprint of Anness Publishing Ltd
Hermes House, 88–89 Blackfriars Road, London SE1 8HA
tel. 020 7401 2077; fax 020 7633 9499
www.southwaterbooks.com; info@anness.com

© Anness Publishing Limited 1999, 2006

UK agent: The Manning Partnership Ltd,
6 The Old Dairy, Melcombe Road,
Bath BA2 3LR; tel. 01225 478444; fax 01225 478440;
sales@manning-partnership.co.uk

UK distributor: Grantham Book Services Ltd, Isaac Newton Way,
Alma Park Industrial Estate, Grantham, Lincs NG31 9SD;
tel. 01476 541080; fax 01476 541061; orders@gbs.tbs-ltd.co.uk

North American agent/distributor: National Book Network,
4501 Forbes Boulevard, Suite 200, Lanham, MD 20706;
tel. 301 459 3366; fax 301 429 5746; www.nbnbooks.com

Australian agent/distributor: Pan Macmillan Australia, Level 18,
St Martins Tower, 31 Market St, Sydney, NSW 2000;
tel. 1300 135 113; fax 1300 135 103;
customer.service@macmillan.com.au

New Zealand agent/distributor: David Bateman Ltd,
30 Tarndale Grove, Off Bush Road, Albany, Auckland;
tel. (09) 415 7664; fax (09) 415 8892

A CIP catalogue is available from the British Library.

Publisher: Joanna Lorenz
Series Editors: Lindsay Porter, Joanne Rippin and Judith Simons
Project Editor: Sarah Ainley
Photographers: James Duncan, John Freeman and Anthony Pickhaver
Designers: Simon Balley, Peter Laws, Lilian Lindblom and Adrian Morris

Additional projects by Petra Boase and Marion Elliot

Previously published as *Outdoor Activities for Kids*

1 2 3 4 5 6 7 8 9 10

contents

introdu

Welcome to the wonderful world of the great outdoors. Take a look

outside and you will see the birds, trees and plants that

live all around you: you see them every day but have you ever

really looked at them before? The natural world is a whole new

adventure just waiting to happen. There are lots of exciting

things to see and do out there, and most of them are right

outside your bedroom window.

It doesn't matter if you live in the city or the countryside – this book will

help you learn to enjoy and look after the world

around us that is called the environment. There are fun

c t i o n

things to do: fascinating nature projects, simple experiments,

things to make, plants to grow and games to play. The best

thing about nature is that you can watch it change every day with the

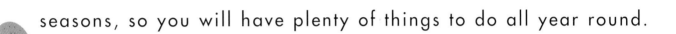

seasons, so you will have plenty of things to do all year round.

In fact there are so many things to do outside we could

hardly fit them all into this book! We hope that what is in here will show you

how to look at the world around you in

a different way, so that you can think

up some fantastic outdoor projects

and games of your own.

Materials and Equipment

Most of the materials and equipment you require for the projects will probably be found in your home. However, always ask someone before taking anything.

Bug box or lens
Use a bug box or lens to see the fascinating microscopic structure of many tiny creatures. Parts of plants such as leaves, seeds and petals can also be viewed in 'close-up'.

Camera and binoculars
These are expensive. They are not essential pieces of equipment, but are useful if you already have them, or can borrow them.

Field guides
These books will help you to identify the animals and plants that you can find. You can borrow them from your local library.

Gardening equipment
Gardening equipment such as bamboo canes, spades and trowels are always useful. They can be used in many nature activities and experiments.

Notebook and pencil
Record the things that you see with a notebook and pencil.

Paints, coloured pens and crayons
Use non-toxic paints and coloured pens to add colour to the drawings in your notebook.

Paper and card (cardboard)
A selection of different types of paper and card (cardboard) are useful for many activities and to display specimens.

Plastic bags
Collect and store specimens in plastic bags. They also stop seeds and young plants from drying out.

Plastic bottles
You can use plastic bottles over and over again. They are used to make several pieces of equipment.

Plastic buckets
Use a bucket to collect water and specimens in.

PVA (white) glue
This type of glue should be used in all projects in this book unless otherwise stated. Glue should be non-toxic and solvent free.

Scissors
Always take care when you use scissors. It is best to have an adult with you when using them. They should have rounded blades.

Sticky labels
Name your specimens on storage boxes and cards.

Sticky tape
Strong sticky tape is useful for making some of the projects.

String
String has many functions. It can be used to make equipment or for measuring things such as a tree trunk.

Supermarket packaging
Re-use plastic pots and boxes, plastic ice cream containers, jars, foam trays, burger boxes, foil dishes, etc. Use them for collecting, storage and making many pieces of equipment.

Tape measure or ruler
These are used to measure specimens and the length of materials you will need.

Torch (flashlight)
This is useful to shine into dark holes and corners and to study animals at night.

Tweezers and paintbrush
You need a steady hand to pick up tiny creatures. A pair of tweezers or a paintbrush will make the job easier.

Other materials used in this book are listed on each page.

bamboo canes

field guide

plastic bucket

notebooks

sticky labels

coloured pens

plastic bottles

plastic bags

paints

crayons

string

scissors

PVA (white) glue

paintbrushes

lens

sticky tape

tweezers

torch
(flashlight)

bug box

tape measure

paper

supermarket
packaging

camera

binoculars

Gardening Equipment

You don't need lots of fancy equipment and you don't need all these tools to start gardening. For many projects just a trowel and hand fork will do, but as you get more enthusiastic, some of these tools will be very useful.

Bamboo canes
Canes are for staking plants, making a compost bin and a wigwam for climbing plants.

Broom
Gardening can be rather like housework because there is always a lot of tidying up to do.

Buckets
Good for collecting weeds and carrying soil, hand tools or even water.

Potting compost
This is used for potting house plants. It will feed your plants the nutrients they need.

Fork
For loosening the soil, and adding compost and manure.

Gardening gloves
Use these to protect your hands from thorns and stinging nettles, and to keep them clean. Try to find a pair that fits properly, if they are too big they can be difficult to work in.

Hand fork
For carefully loosening the soil between plants in small flower beds and for window boxes.

Hoe
For weeding. It slices like a knife under the roots of weeds which then shrivel up and die.

Penknife
Often useful instead of scissors.

Rake
For making a level surface.

Scissors
Used mainly for cutting garden twine, but useful for snipping off all sorts of things.

Secateurs (clippers)
For cutting off plant stems and small branches.

Seed tray
Seed trays are used for sowing seeds and growing seedlings.

Spade
For turning over the soil by digging and for making holes for planting trees and shrubs.

Trowel
A mini spade for making small holes and digging up big weeds.

Twine
This is gardening string for tying plants, and for marking out a straight line.

Watering can
A very important piece of equipment as without water plants die quickly. Immediately after planting always water thoroughly with the sprinkler for a gentle rain-like shower.

Wheelbarrow
For carting all sorts of things round the garden.

Wire
Useful for holding plants against walls and fences. Little pieces are used for pegging down.

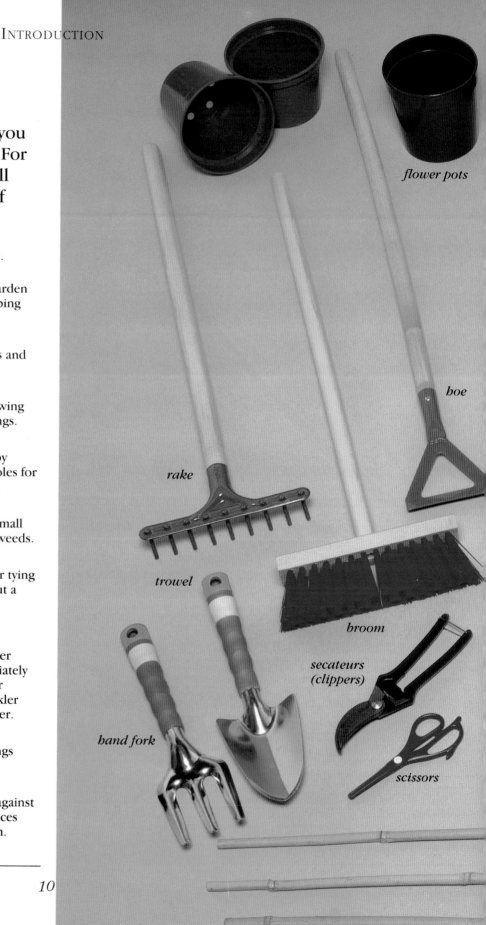

flower pots

hoe

rake

trowel

broom

secateurs (clippers)

hand fork

scissors

seed tray

wheelbarrow

spade

wire

buckets

fork   gloves

compost

twine

penknife   watering can

bamboo canes

Soil care

Soil is made from bits of rock and all sorts of plant and animal remains. It is wonderful stuff and without it, no plants could grow and no people or animals could survive, so it is worth taking care of!

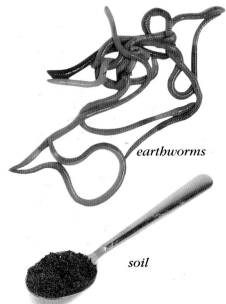

earthworms

soil

HEALTHY SOIL

Healthy soil is teeming with wildlife. Many animals are so small that you cannot see them. In fact there are billions of busy minute animals in every teaspoonful of soil.

Earthworms and beetles are appreciated for their good work. They create tunnels that allow air and water in, and surplus water to drain out. They eat loads of leaves and bits of plants, and turn them into very rich compost which is food for plants.

The soil is a living thing and, like the plants growing in it and all other living things, it needs looking after.

leaves

leaf mould

DIGGING AND FORKING

Digging and forking the soil lets in air which is important for the plants' roots and for all the animals living in the soil. Never work on the soil when it is wet because it can turn into mud without any air. Dig or fork the soil by turning it over down to a depth of about 30 cm (12 in). Break up all the large lumps but leave the surface level.

When you are gardening, try not to walk on the soft soil around your plants, because that squashes out the air too.

manure

compost

fertilizer

Fertilizers contain plant foods, and there are many different sorts that come in the form of granules, powders or liquids. It always says clearly on the packet the type of plant it should be used for and how you should apply it.

A mulch is a thick layer of manure or garden compost, which is put on the surface of the soil around plants. In a year's time it will have virtually disappeared, but in the meantime it has fed and conditioned the soil and stopped any weeds growing.

THE MAGIC OF MANURE AND COMPOST

The soil, like every living thing, needs feeding. In nature leaves fall and plants and animals die and decay. In the garden we need to add manure, compost and fertilizers.

Manure is rotted-down bedding and droppings from animals like horses and cows that have a vegetarian diet. It is wonderful stuff for the soil because it helps to hold water and keeps the soil loose. It is also very rich in plant foods.

If you don't have any farms or stables near you, garden compost is just as good as manure and is something everyone can make. Use some sort of container to collect vegetable peelings from the kitchen, and prunings and soft weeds from the garden. Piled into a heap, they rot down in a few months, making stuff that looks like soil but is a feast for all kinds of plants.

Use manure and garden compost to fork into the soil and into planting holes. For perfect plants and to save on weeding, pile as much as you can around the plants after planting. This is called a mulch and is the best gift of all for soil and plants.

Safety First

Here are a few important things to remember to protect yourself and the animals and plants in the countryside around you.

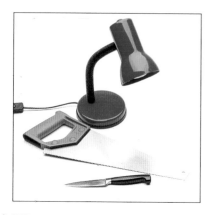

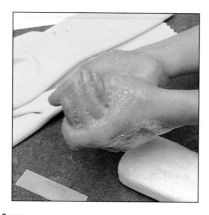

! **1** Sharp knives, tools and electricity are dangerous to use. Always ask an adult to help you with these.

! **2** Some animals can carry harmful germs. Always wash your hands after touching them. Germs also live in rivers and ponds. If you have cut your hand, put a plaster (band-aid) on it and wear rubber gloves before pond and river dipping. Always wash your hands afterwards.

! **3** Don't fall in! Be extremely careful near water, rivers, slippery rocks, sea, strong currents and soft mud. If it looks dangerous, do not go near it! Always ask an adult that you know and trust to come with you if you are out at night, or visiting wild and lonely places.

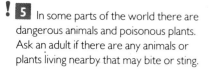

! **4** Some strong glue and paint can give off harmful fumes. Always use them in a well ventilated place, preferably outside. Always read the manufacturers' labels.

! **5** In some parts of the world there are dangerous animals and poisonous plants. Ask an adult if there are any animals or plants living nearby that may bite or sting.

! **6** Many fungi are poisonous. Do not touch any of them unless a qualified adult tells you that they are safe.

! **7** Many berries are also poisonous. Ask an adult to show you which ones are safe to eat or touch.

Country Code

Follow these simple rules for care and safety of the environment.

2 Return logs and rocks to the original position that you found them in. This will preserve the microhabitat (home) for the animals living underneath.

1 Don't pick wildflowers unless you have permission; it is illegal in many countries. Draw or photograph them instead.

4 Shut gates and keep to footpaths. Follow land-owners' instructions.

3 Keep your dog on a lead (leash) near farm animals.

!5 Be careful not to start fires. A dropped cigarette, broken glass or a barbeque can start a forest fire. Miles of habitat are destroyed and thousands of animals die in forest fires.

6 Take litter home. It looks ugly and can harm or kill many wild animals.

Collecting and Recording

The easiest way to study nature is simply to look and listen. But, if you write down the things that you see, you will remember them afterwards. Make a nature notebook or diary and you will soon see how things change throughout the year.

YOU WILL NEED
notebook
pencil
coloured pens

pencil

notebook

coloured pens

Date	Place	Weather	Habitat
6th May	oak woods	cloudy	Mixed woodland oak + beech
Sunday 15th June	Walk to Lilypond	breezy	Shallow lake - lots of waterplants.
Sunday 30th July	Sandy View beach	Hot and sunny	sand rocks rockpools.
Mon 3rd	Walk to Tom's	rainy	playing fields - grass, hedges around
Sunday 5th Sept.	picnic - Fairview Farm	sunny, few clouds	grassy meadow and fields.

1 Every time you go out, you visit a habitat. This is the place where animals and plants live. It may be a park, a garden, a wood or by a lake.

2 In your notebook you should make a list and write about the different habitats that you have seen.

Tree	Flower	Bird	Mammal
oak	daisy	jay	rabbit
fir	orchid	robin	squirrel
beech			

3 Each time that you go out, make a list of the different types of animals and plants that you see. Each type of animal or plant is called a species.

4 Certain animals and plants are often found together. These bees are feeding on knapweed. Write the following in your notebook: Where did you see the animals? What or who are they with? What are they doing?

5 Sometimes you will see something unusual, like this fairy mushroom ring. Write about it and draw or photograph it. Stick your photographs and postcards into your notebook later.

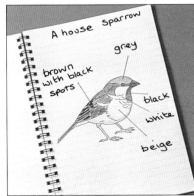

6 You may sometimes see an animal or bird that you do not recognize. Make a drawing of it in your notebook. Then you can identify it with a field guide when you get home. Make a note of different colours and patterns and write about where it was and what it was doing.

At last, winter is over: the days are getting longer, the weather is warmer and you feel like you want to run outside after all those weekends stuck indoors. Look closely and you will see the amazing changes taking place around you as the natural world wakes from its long winter sleep. Leaves burst out on the trees, bright spring flowers push up through the ground, birds prepare their nests and animals come out of hibernation. This is a very exciting time of year – so go outside and enjoy it!

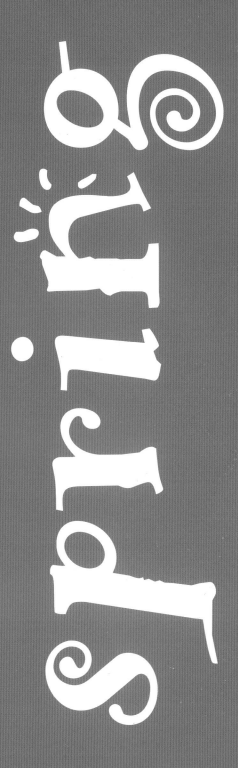

spring

Plaster Casts

Animals often leave their footprints in soft mud and sand. Make plaster casts of them to keep a permanent record. You can paint them when the plaster is dry.

YOU WILL NEED
strip of card (cardboard)
paperclip
plaster of Paris
water
bucket or plastic tub
spoon
small trowel
old brush or toothbrush (optional)

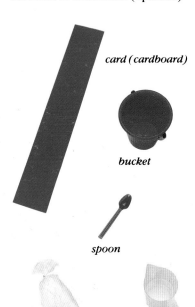

card (cardboard)

bucket

spoon

plaster of Paris

water

paperclips

1 Look for animal footprints in mud and sand.

2 Select the clearest footprint.

3 Put the card (cardboard) around the print and secure with a paperclip. Push the card down slightly into the mud.

4 Next, mix the plaster of Paris. Put a small amount of water into the bucket. Add plaster powder and stir well.

5 Pour the plaster into the mould and leave to set.

6 Once set, use a small trowel to dig up the plaster and print. Clean off the soil and sand. You may need to use an old brush or toothbrush to clean into all the small cracks.

Tracking Snails

Garden snails sleep together in a big cluster called a rookery. They often return to the same place to sleep day after day.

YOU WILL NEED
child's peel-off nail polish
flowerpot
small stone

stone

flowerpot

nail polish

1 Search in a garden or park for a group of sleeping snails.

2 You will find them clustered together under logs, rocks or bricks.

3 Pick out 10 snails. Put a small dot of nail polish on each of their shells.

4 Collect your marked snails. Put them under an upturned flowerpot nearby. Put a stone under the rim of the flowerpot so that the snails can crawl out. The next morning, see if you can find the snails. Are they still under the flowerpot?

NATURE TIP
After you have found the snails, gently peel off the nail polish, otherwise the bright colour will attract the birds.

Keeping Slugs and Snails

Slugs and snails can be kept in a tank. Here, you can learn how to make them a comfortable home.

YOU WILL NEED
gravel
small tank or large plastic
    ice cream container
soil
moss and grass
small stones, pieces of bark and
    dried leaves
gauze or netting
string
scissors

small tank

gauze

string

soil

gravel

moss

stone, bark and dried leaves

1 Put a layer of gravel in the bottom of the tank or container.

2 Cover the gravel with a layer of soil.

NATURE TIP

Keep your snails in a cool place. Feed them on a small amount of breakfast cereal (not too sugary), and small pieces of fruit and vegetables. Add fresh grass and leaves when needed.

3 Plant pieces of moss and grass in the soil. Add stones, bark and the dried leaves. Water the tank just enough to moisten the soil.

4 Put in a few slugs or snails and cover the tank with a piece of gauze or netting. Tie it down with string or replace the lid. Make sure that it has plenty of air holes.

Keeping Caterpillars

This is a nice clean way to keep caterpillars.
Eventually they will turn into pupae and then
into beautiful butterflies and moths.

YOU WILL NEED
collecting pot
plastic bottle
scissors
paper towels
large jar
sticky tape
gauze or netting
rubber band or string

plastic bottle

collecting pot

gauze

scissors

sticky tape

rubber band

1 Look for some caterpillars living on cabbages and other plants. Put them in a collecting pot. At the same time, collect some leaves from the plants that you found the caterpillars living on.

2 Cut the bottom from the plastic bottle with a pair of scissors.

3 Take a bunch of leaves and foliage that you found the caterpillars on. Wrap a piece of paper towel around the stalks of the leaves.

4 Put the leaves inside the bottle and push the stalks through the neck so that the tissue forms a plug.

5 Stand the bottle neck-down in a jar of water. Make sure that the plant stalks are standing in the water. Tape the bottle to the jar if it is wobbly and does not stand firmly.

NATURE TIP

Every few days, clean out the bottle, wash it, dry it, and give the caterpillars fresh plants to eat. Eventually the caterpillars will pupate. They will turn into sausage-shaped pupae. You can keep them until the butterflies or moths emerge, and then you must release them outside.

6 Put the caterpillars inside the bottle. Cover the top with a piece of gauze. Hold it in place with a rubber band or tie with string. Feed your caterpillars regularly.

Making a Plankton Net

This net is used to catch tiny water creatures that would pass through the holes in a normal fishing net.

YOU WILL NEED
thick wire
old pair of tights (panty hose)
scissors
long bamboo cane
string
small plastic jar

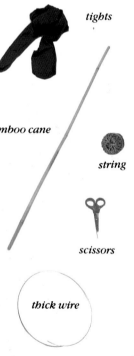

tights

bamboo cane

string

scissors

thick wire

plastic jar

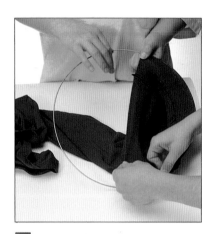

1 Thread the wire through the waist of the tights.

2 Cut the legs off the tights.

3 Twist the ends of the wire together.

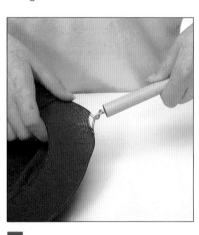

4 Push the twisted wires into the end of the cane.

5 Use string to tie the bottom of the net around the neck of the jar. Tie as tightly as you can.

6 When you use this net the pond animals are caught in the jar at the bottom.

Pond and River Dipping

Beneath the surface of the water lives a rich and varied animal and plant life. Dip into the world of a pond or river using a fishing or plankton net and discover the creatures that live there.

YOU WILL NEED
ice cream container or bucket
fishing and/or plankton net
shallow white dishes, made by cutting
  the top from an ice cream container
paintbrush
jam jar or tank
notebook
pencil

net

jam jar

pencil

notebook

ice cream container

paintbrush

1 Fill an ice cream container or bucket with pond water. You will then have something to put your animals in as soon as you catch them.

2 Sweep the fishing or plankton net through the weeds.

3 Pour the water from the plankton net into an ice cream container or bucket by pushing the jar up through the net. Pull the net back and pour the water out.

4 You will soon catch many different animals. Here are two types of pond snail – a round Ramshorn Snail and a pointed Greater Pond Snail.

5 Carefully pick out the animals you have just caught with a paintbrush and place them into a clean shallow dish or ice cream container, of water. You will have caught a lot of rubbish such as dead leaves, and the clean water will help you see the animals more clearly.

!SAFETY TIP
Take care around water, no matter
how shallow it seems.

6 You can also put them into a large
jam jar, or small tank. Identify the species
you have found and make notes in your
notebook. Visit different ponds, lakes, and
rivers. Do you find the same species living
in different places?

Beach Transect

Many creatures make their home on the beach, but we have to search hard to find them. The sea comes up and down the beach with the tides, so different animals and plants are found at different levels of the beach – from the top to the bottom, nearest to the sea. A transect is a way of measuring these changes.

YOU WILL NEED
long roll of string
bamboo canes
notebook
pencil

pencil

notebook

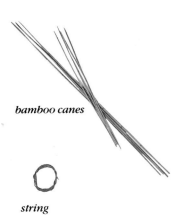

bamboo canes

string

1 Take a long piece of string and stretch it from the top of the beach towards the sea. Use bamboo canes to hold the string up. Starting from the top of the beach, walk along the string towards the sea. Every 50 paces, stop and write down all the animals and plants that you can find at each place in your nature notebook.

!SAFETY TIP

Take care on slippery rocks. Do not get cut off by incoming tides.

2 At the top of the beach (as close to the land as possible), you will find a few types of land plants that can live in these salty places.

3 The strandline (high tide line) is the highest place reached by the high tide. Sandhoppers and seaweed flies live here.

4 On the upper shore you will find green seaweed.

5 The middle shore is often covered by wide banks of brown seaweed called wrack (rockweed) and by barnacles covering the rocks.

6 You are on the lower shore when you find red seaweed and large brown seaweed called kelp attached to rocks. This part of the shore is only exposed at low tide and is where you will find most animals living.

Sowing Seeds Indoors

Many plants that are grown for their summer flowers come from warm parts of the world. To grow them in countries with colder climates, they have to be started off indoors and only planted outside when there are no more frosts.

GARDENER'S TIP
Don't forget to write the name of the seeds on a label and stick it in so that you don't forget what you've planted.

YOU WILL NEED
seed or potting compost (soil)
seed tray
small flower pot with flat bottom
seeds
shallow seed tray

shallow seed tray

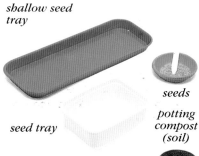

seeds

seed tray

potting compost (soil)

flower pot

1 Use seed or potting compost (soil) to fill a seed tray. Overfill it, then knock the compost (soil) level and use a small pot with a flat bottom to press the surface down slightly to level it all over.

2 Sow the seeds, spacing them out carefully with about 1 cm (½ in) between each seed.

3 Cover the seeds with a little compost (soil), just enough so you cannot see them any more.

4 To water the seeds without disturbing them, stand the seed tray in a shallow seed tray of water so it soaks the compost (soil) up from the bottom. Add a little water at a time, when the compost (soil) is wet enough, it will feel heavy and you will see the moisture glistening on the surface.

Pricking Out (Thinning)

When seeds have germinated and grown a few leaves, they need to be moved so they can be given space to grow bigger.

YOU WILL NEED
small flower pot
potting compost (soil)
small stick
watering can

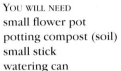

watering can

flower pot

stick

potting compost (soil)

1 Fill a small pot with compost (soil). Level and firm it lightly.

2 With one hand use a small stick to lever the seedling out of the compost (soil), and hold the seedling by a seed leaf with the other.

3 Move the seedling to the pot and use the stick to make a hole, which should be deep enough for the roots to fit in comfortably.

4 Place the seedling in the hole and press some potting compost (soil) lightly against the roots. Be very careful, they are very delicate. Water in, using a watering can with a sprinkler on the end to give a gentle shower.

DID YOU KNOW?

The first pair of leaves at the bottom are called the seed leaves. They usually look different from the others and are used by the young seedlings to give them the first boost of energy to get growing.

Making a Seed Bed

A seed bed is easy to make when you know how and have had a bit of practice. It is important to make it as level as possible so that the tiny seeds can reach the small soil particles to get food and water as soon as possible.

YOU WILL NEED
spade or fork
rake
bamboo cane
short stick
seeds

bamboo cane

spade

rake

stick

seeds

1 Use a spade or fork to turn over the soil, working in a straight line. Knock out any large lumps and take out any weeds and stones as you go.

2 To get a level surface, the soil needs to be firm. Do a duck walk up and down, pressing in with your heels on the forked-over soil.

3 Use a rake to make it level. Pull it gently backwards and forwards, and flick out any remaining stones.

Sowing Outside

Some plants need to be sown indoors because they are not hardy enough to grow outside. Others can be sown straight into the ground, but read the packet to make sure you are sowing at the right time of the year. To sow outside, you need to make a seed drill.

GARDENER'S TIP
Don't forget to write a label and stick it in at the end of the row.

1 To make a seed drill, put something with a straight edge (like a bamboo cane) onto the prepared soil. Then use a short stick to mark out a groove against it, about 2 cm (³/₄ in) deep.

2 Place large seeds into the drill, at least 1 cm (¹/₂ in) apart. Small seeds should be sprinkled evenly pinch-by-pinch on a day when there isn't much wind.

3 Cover them over with soil by hand and pat it down gently.

4 When you have covered all the seeds, water thoroughly with the sprinkler on your watering can. Make sure the water comes out gently or you will move the seeds in their bed.

Weed-out

Weeds are very clever and successful plants which make the most of every opportunity that comes their way. Some, such as dandelions and alkanet, have very long, fleshy roots that can grow from the smallest piece left in the ground. Others, such as bindweed, have tough leathery roots that snake through the soil, and twining stems which grow so quickly that they take over everything in sight.

LONG-LIVED WEEDS

You have to work really hard to get rid of these. Dig right down into the soil using a spade or trowel to get out as much root as you can.

Nettle
Everyone knows this plant because of its stinging hairs, but did you know that there are two types? The smaller one lives for only a short time and has white roots, while the larger one lives for several years, and has spreading stems that creep along the soil and roots that are yellow. The smaller one can easily be pulled up using gloves, but the larger one needs a little more patience to dig up the long roots and creeping stems. Watch out, they both sting!

Bindweed
This is a real nuisance because it can regrow from just the tiniest piece of root left in the soil. It climbs with twining stems that choke out everything else.

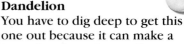

Alkanet
This weed has pretty blue flowers but it is a bully in a flower bed, and will eventually take over. It has a long, thick tap root like a dandelion so it is difficult to dig out.

Dandelion
You have to dig deep to get this one out because it can make a new plant from the smallest piece left in the soil. The well-known dandelion "clock" is the seed head which gets blown about by the wind.

Oxalis

This has very pretty flowers, but don't be fooled, it is one of the most difficult weeds to get rid of. It grows from small bulbils growing underground, which must be dug up and carefully thrown away. Don't put them on the compost heap, otherwise you will spread them around even more.

Sow thistle

The best way to get rid of this in flower and vegetable beds is to hoe it or pull it up. The seeds are very light and have a plume of hairs which carries them in the wind. If you break the stem, it has a milky juice.

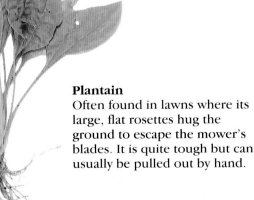

Plantain

Often found in lawns where its large, flat rosettes hug the ground to escape the mower's blades. It is quite tough but can usually be pulled out by hand.

SHORT-LIVED WEEDS

Many of these can be pulled out by hand or, using a hoe, by chopping off the roots and leaving the tops to shrivel and die. These are weeds spread by seeds, so catch them before they flower and do more damage.

Groundsel

This seems to pop up everywhere, but at least it is easy to pull up. Try and catch it before it makes seeds.

Mercury

Another weed that quickly seeds itself almost anywhere, but it can easily be pulled up or hoed off.

Shepherd's purse

A little weed that is very quick-growing. It has triangular seeds which get sticky when wet and can be carried around on boots and tools. Each plant can produce up to 4,000 seeds in one year that can survive in the soil for up to 30 years!

Bugs: the Good, the Bad and the Ugly

Bugs can be gardeners' friends as well as enemies, so it is important to recognize the good guys like ladybird and lacewing larvae, as well as the baddies.

Here are some of the most common and important bugs which you will find in your garden. Encourage the insects which are on your side to stay by creating the right environment for them. Don't be frightened of them! They're much smaller than you and each one has an important role to play in the life of a garden.

Examine your garden for these insects and find out who lives where.

THE GOOD

Butterfly and bee tub.

Bees
Without bees we would have hardly any fruit or vegetables because they play the vital role of pollinating the flowers.

Beetles
Beetles scurry around at night feeding on the small insects and slugs that feed on your plants.

Lacewings
These pretty insects have see-through lacy wings, and the larvae feed on plant-eating greenflies (aphids).

Ladybirds
Both the ladybird itself and its larvae feed greedily on greenfly (aphids) and help to keep them under control.

Encourage lacewings to stay in your garden by making them somewhere to live.

THE BAD

Caterpillars
Caterpillars feed hungrily on all sorts of plants. If they are on your cabbages, you might want to get rid of them. However, many caterpillars are fascinating to watch and they do turn into beautiful moths and butterflies.

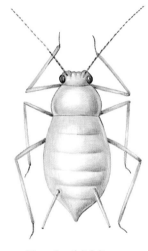

Greenflies (aphids)
Greenflies (aphids) have pointed mouths with which they pierce the leaves and stems of plants and suck out the sap. The plants then become misshapen and weak.

A blast of water will help to reduce the numbers – soapy water is best. The trouble with a lot of chemical sprays is that they kill all the good guys too, who would normally help to keep the greenflies (aphids) under control.

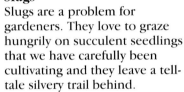

Slugs
Slugs are a problem for gardeners. They love to graze hungrily on succulent seedlings that we have carefully been cultivating and they leave a tell-tale silvery trail behind.

The best way to control them is to go out at night when they are feeding, pick them off and drop them in a pot of salty water. Or buy some slug pellets.

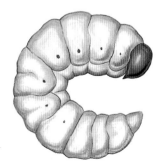

Vine weevil
This is a baddie, no doubt about it! The adult weevil lives a secretive life feeding on the leaves of plants, but it is their larvae that do the real damage.

They feed off the roots of plants, usually of those growing in pots and containers although they can sometimes be found in flower beds too.

Plants being attacked start to wilt, then topple over as soon as you touch them because they have no roots left. If you find any, immediately throw away all the compost or soil that the affected plant was growing in.

THE UGLY

Lily beetle
Lily beetles are often left alone because they are a pretty bright red colour. Their larvae, however, are one of the ugliest things around. They are covered in a horrible jelly-like mucus which protects them.

Both the adult beetles and the larvae feed on lily leaves and stems and can quickly strip a plant so watch out for them!

Sprouting Seeds

How do you grow fresh vegetables at any time of the year without having a garden? Sprouting seeds. They grow quickly, are very good for you and taste delicious too, so who could ask for more? These bean sprouts are grown from mung beans, but other dried seeds like chickpeas (garbanzo beans) and whole lentils work well too. For the quickest results try tiny alfalfa seeds. All these are easy to buy from any health food shop and many supermarkets.

YOU WILL NEED
flat-bottomed dish
cotton wool or kitchen paper towel
mung beans
newspaper

newspaper

mung beans

flat-bottomed dish

cotton wool

1 Wash the beans and soak them overnight in cold water.

2 Next morning, cover a flat-bottomed dish with a layer of cotton wool, or several sheets of kitchen paper towels, and water.

3 Wash the beans again and spread them evenly over the damp bottom of the dish.

4 Cover the dish with newspaper to keep out light and put it in a warm place. The beans will soon sprout and be ready to eat in 6-9 days. Don't let them grow too long, they should be plump and about 2.5 cm (1 in) long for the best taste.

VARIATION

Another way of sprouting larger seeds is to put a large spoonful of dry seeds such as chickpeas (garbanzo beans) into a wide-necked jar and cover with a small piece of muslin (cheesecloth), secured by an elastic band. Fill the jar with water and swish the seeds around a bit, then pour the water out. Do this at least once every day (twice if you can) to stop them going bad. They will take between 2-7 days to sprout, depending on what type you are growing.

DID YOU KNOW?

To cook bean sprouts, wash them, then boil in a pan of salted water for 2 minutes. Drain, and serve with butter and a few drops of soy sauce.

Cunning Cuttings

Early in the year, fresh young shoots are bursting with energy and can be cut off and persuaded to make roots. Try taking cuttings of lots of different plants – some are easier than others but you won't know until you try.

YOU WILL NEED
small shallow flower pot
potting compost (soil)
penknife or scissors
fuchsia
plastic bag
piece of string

fuchsia

flower pot

potting compost (soil)

piece of string

penknife

plastic bag

DID YOU KNOW?
The plastic bag helps to keep the air moist around the leaves, while the cuttings make roots to grow away on their own.

! SAFETY NOTE
Always take great care when using any sharp objects.

1 Fill a small shallow flower pot either with ordinary (regular) potting compost (soil) or, even better, one that is specially mixed for cuttings.

3 Gently take off the lower pair of leaves, being careful not to tear the stem.

2 Using a penknife or scissors, cut off a shoot tip which is at least 5 cm (2 in) long and which has three sets of leaves

4 Make a hole in the compost (soil) and put the cutting in. Then press the compost (soil) lightly against the stem. Fill the pot with a few more cuttings, spacing them about 3 cm (1½ in) apart.

GARDENER'S TIP
If you don't have any potting compost (soil), it is often possible to root cuttings in a glass of water. After a couple of weeks in one pot the cuttings will need more space and should be gently moved to pots of their own.

from the fuchsia. Then make a clean, straight cut just below where a pair of leaves joins the stem.

5 Give the pot a good watering then put it in a plastic bag and tie the top together with string. Place on a light windowsill and watch a new plant grow!

A Sunny Spot and a Shady One

There is a plant for every place in the garden and neither bright sun nor a bit of shade is any problem. Here are two little gardens, one for the sun and one for the shade.

A SUNNY SPOT

Hot dry places are not ideal for every plant but some, like marigolds, petunias and cosmeas (cosmos), absolutely love it. Grey-leafed plants like cotton lavender, usually come from warm countries and always do well in hot sunny places. Follow steps 1 and 2 for a shady spot to prepare the ground for this sunny garden.

YOU WILL NEED
trowel
cosmeas (cosmos)
cotton lavender or other grey-
 leaved plant
petunias
marigolds

marigold   *cosmeas (cosmos)*

petunias   *trowel*

1 When you have prepared the ground plant the cosmea seedlings at the back. They grow over a metre (3 feet) tall so they need the most space.

2 Plant the cotton lavender, which has lovely yellow flowers in early summer, in front of the cosmeas (cosmos).

3 Plant the petunias and marigolds in the front of the bed. Water thoroughly.

GARDENER'S TIP
Be sure to take off all the faded marigold and petunia flowers before they make seeds, that way they will dazzle you with colour for months.

A SHADY SPOT

All sorts of plants will flourish in a shady flower bed, but for colour all summer long, it is difficult to beat a combination of fuchsias and busy lizzies (patience plants). You could also use primroses, lilies and ferns.

YOU WILL NEED
compost or fertilizer
trowel
fuchsia
busy lizzies
 (patience plants)
woodruff seeds

*busy lizzies
(patience plants)*

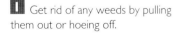

*woodruff
seeds*

fuchsia

trowel

1 Get rid of any weeds by pulling them out or hoeing off.

2 Fork over the soil and give it a boost by forking in a generous helping of good garden compost or manure, or a handful of fertilizer.

3 Start by planting the tallest plant, the fuchsia, at the back. Use a trowel to dig a hole that is slightly deeper than the pot, ease the fuchsia out of its pot and plant it in the hole.

4 Plant the busy lizzies (patience plants) around the fuchsia, spacing them about 20 cm (8 in) apart. Sprinkle the woodruff seeds in the gaps. Water the garden thoroughly.

Growing Wildflowers

Wildflowers are easy to grow from seed and can be very attractive in your garden. They will encourage more insects to visit them, who will in turn attract more birds to your garden.

YOU WILL NEED
seed tray or flowerpot
soil
packet of wildflower seeds
plastic bag

seed tray

soil

plastic bag

1 Fill the seed tray or flowerpot with a layer of soil.

2 Sprinkle on the seeds.

3 Cover the seeds with a layer of soil.

4 Water, and then cover the seed tray or pot with a plastic bag. Leave on a windowsill.

5 When the seedlings have sprouted, remove the plastic bag. Water regularly. As they grow larger, plant the seedlings into larger flowerpots or directly into your garden.

The Tallest Sunflower

Sunflowers are one of the speediest plants to grow in your garden. In just 6 months they outstrip everything else and can easily grow up to 3 metres (10 ft) tall.

They need some sort of support to stop them blowing over in windy weather. Plant them against a wall or fence that you can tie them to, or use a tall bamboo cane.

YOU WILL NEED
small flower pot
potting compost (soil)
sunflower seeds
watering can
a very tall bamboo cane – at least
  2 m (6 ft)
string

flower pots   *sunflower seeds*

*potting compost
(soil)*

bamboo canes

string

1 Fill the flower pots with compost (soil) and sow 2 or 3 seeds about 1 cm (½ in) deep. Water them in using a watering can with a sprinkler on the end.

2 When the seeds have germinated, pull out all but the strongest seedling in each pot.

3 Keep the pots on a sunny window sill until the seedlings have grown and the weather is warm, then plant outside.

4 Put the cane in the soil and tie it loosely to the plant. Measure the height of the plant when the flower appears.

Lovely Lilies

Few flowers have as much going for them as lilies. They are exotic, colourful and often heavily scented. They are also easy to grow and are perfect for planting in pots. Be sure to buy only fat, healthy bulbs with thick, fleshy roots.

YOU WILL NEED
pebbles
large flower pot
potting compost (soil)
3 lily bulbs

potting compost (soil)

flower pot

pebbles

lily bulbs

1 Put a layer of pebbles in the bottom of a large flower pot so that water can drain away easily.

2 Fill the pot half full with potting compost (soil).

GARDENER'S TIP
When the flowers die cut them off. Let the leaves die and in autumn (fall) replant the bulbs into fresh compost and they will grow all over again!

3 Plant the lily bulbs, taking great care of the roots, and spacing the bulbs evenly in the pot.

4 Cover with compost (soil), finishing a little way below the rim of the pot, then water them well.

Blooming Old Boots

Don't these look great? It is a blooming wonderful way to recycle an old pair of boots, the bigger the better. It just goes to show that almost anything can be used to grow plants in as long as it has a few holes in the bottom for drainage. Try an old football, a sports bag, or even an old hat, for plant containers with lots of character.

! SAFETY NOTE
Always take great care when using any sharp objects.

YOU WILL NEED
knife
old pair of working boots
potting compost (soil)
selection of bedding plants
watering can

knife

bedding plants

watering can

potting compost (soil)

old boot

1 Using a knife very carefully (in fact you will probably need help), make some holes in between the stitching of the sole for drainage. Even better if there are holes there naturally!

2 Fill the boots with potting compost (soil), pushing it down right into the toe.

3 Plant flowers that can cope with hot, dry places like geraniums and verbenas which will trail over the edge.

5 The boot needs watering every day in the summer, and blooms even better if you mix some plant food in to the water once a week.

4 Squeeze in a pansy with a contrasting flower colour, and a trailing lobelia plant. Lobelia grows in the smallest of spaces and will delicately tumble over the edge.

Sweet Sweet Peas

Few flowers smell sweeter than sweet peas. They have a floaty, delicate perfume and an amazing array of colours. The most important thing about growing them is that you must cut the flowers every day to stop seeds developing, that way they will keep flowering for a lot longer. I can think of worse jobs to do, can't you? The seedlings have long, delicate roots so an ideal pot is a long one that is made out of newspaper. It can be planted and left in the soil so the roots are not disturbed.

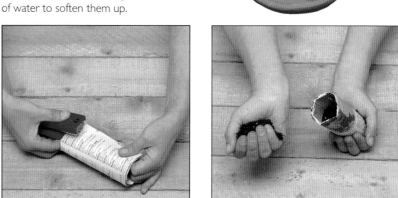

1 Sweet pea seeds have very hard skins, so soak them overnight in a saucer of water to soften them up.

YOU WILL NEED
sweet pea seeds
small saucer of water
newspaper
stapler
potting compost (soil)
plastic carton
trowel

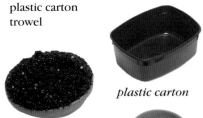

plastic carton

potting compost (soil)

stapler

sweet pea seeds

newspaper

2 The next morning fold a double sheet of newspaper into 3.

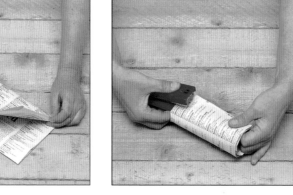

3 Then roll it up to make a tube and staple it together in several places.

4 Hold one hand under one end and fill with potting compost (soil).

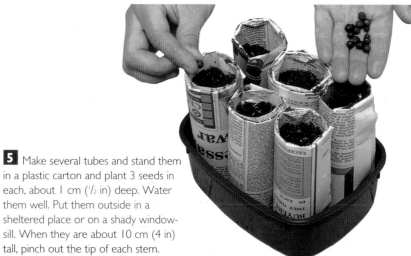

5 Make several tubes and stand them in a plastic carton and plant 3 seeds in each, about 1 cm (½ in) deep. Water them well. Put them outside in a sheltered place or on a shady window-sill. When they are about 10 cm (4 in) tall, pinch out the tip of each stem.

6 Plant them outside in the spring, against some wire netting or canes for them to climb up. Water often.

! SAFETY NOTE
Always take great care when using any sharp objects.

A Bag of Potatoes

Home-grown potatoes taste ten times better than bought ones, and nothing could be easier to grow. Start them off early in the year using potatoes either from your vegetable rack at home, or, better still, using special seed potatoes from a garden centre. When the plant starts flowering the potatoes are ready for harvesting. This is about 10-12 weeks after planting.

YOU WILL NEED
seed potatoes
egg box
strong, dark coloured plastic bag
potting compost (soil)
sharp object to make holes in bag

potting compost (soil)

screwdriver

egg box

seed potatoes

plastic bag

❗ SAFETY NOTE
Always take great care when using any sharp objects.

1 To help your potatoes get off to a speedy start, put them in an egg box with the end that has the most eyes pointing upwards. This is where the baby shoots will grow from. Place the box on a cool but light windowsill and leave for a few weeks until the first signs of life appear – little fat green leaves.

2 Fill the plastic bag one-third full of potting compost (soil), and make a few holes with a screwdriver in the bottom so that excess water can drain through.

3 Plant 2 or 3 potatoes in the bag, with their shoots pointing upwards.

4 Cover them over with potting compost (soil) so you end up with the bag half full. Give the bag a good water and put it outside, in a sheltered place where it will not get caught by a frost.

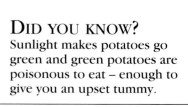

5 After several weeks when the shoots are between 15 and 30 cm (6 and 12 in) tall, add more compost (soil) so the bag is completely full. This is called earthing up and it encourages the stems to make more potatoes as well as stopping light getting to them.

DID YOU KNOW?
Sunlight makes potatoes go green and green potatoes are poisonous to eat – enough to give you an upset tummy.

Wigwam Runners

Runner beans are climbing plants and need something to run up, so a wigwam is just the thing. This looks just as good in a flower bed as in a vegetable garden. The flowers are pretty and are followed by long, tasty beans which, if you pick them every few days, will grow all summer.

YOU WILL NEED
fork
manure or garden compost
5 x 2 m (6 ft) bamboo canes
garden string
runner bean seeds

garden string

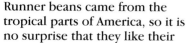

runner bean seeds

bamboo canes

compost

DID YOU KNOW?
Runner beans came from the tropical parts of America, so it is no surprise that they like their roots to be in warm soil. They also grow fast – you could have a plate of beans in just 7 weeks!

1 At the end of spring, when the days are warm and there are no more frosts, fork over a patch of soil. Add a bucketful of manure or well-rotted garden compost and mix it in well.

2 Push 5 long bamboo canes into the ground, in a circle measuring roughly 1 m (3 ft) across the middle.

3 Gather the canes together at the top and tie with a piece of string to make a wigwam shape.

4 Plant a seed about 3 cm (1¼ in) deep on both sides of each cane. Water thoroughly. They will soon germinate and start to run up the canes. When they reach the top, pinch out the top few centimetres (inches) of the stem.

Tomatoes in a Bag

Grow-bags are great for growing tomatoes in because they provide almost everything the plant needs. You can buy the bags in most garden centres. The plastic funnel acts as a mini reservoir and makes watering and feeding much easier.

YOU WILL NEED
scissors
1 grow-bag
3 tomato plants
2 bamboo canes
garden twine
large plastic bottle

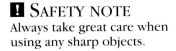
plastic bottle

tomato plant
garden twine
scissors
grow-bag
bamboo canes

! SAFETY NOTE
Always take great care when using any sharp objects.

1 Make drainage holes in the bottom of the grow-bag and cut out the squares marked in the plastic by the dotted lines. Make a hole in each square and plant one of the tomato plants.

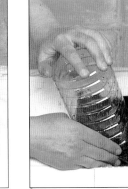

2 Push a bamboo cane into each square and tie the plant to it loosely.

3 Cut the bottom off the plastic bottle to make a funnel shape. Plant the funnel next to the plant and fill with water.

DID YOU KNOW?
Tall-growing types of tomato should only be allowed to develop one main stem. Lots of side shoots will try to grow in between where the leaves meet the main stem, and these should be picked off as soon as you spot them.

GARDENER'S TIP
Keep the tomatoes well watered and as soon as flowers appear, feed once a week as well with a special tomato fertilizer that is high in potassium which is important for all fruits.

side shoot

Good Enough to Eat!

You don't need a large garden to grow fruit and vegetables – it is possible to grow some in just a window box. Strawberries and bush or trailing types of tomatoes are small enough, so are radishes and lettuces.

GARDENER'S TIP
To get a plant out of a pot, turn it upside down with the stem between your fingers. With the other hand, firmly squeeze the bottom of the pot to loosen it.

YOU WILL NEED
window box
potting compost (soil)
tomato plants
strawberry plants
radish seeds
lettuce seeds
nasturtium seeds

DID YOU KNOW?
Nasturtium leaves and flowers are edible, with a hot, peppery taste. They look lovely on a plate of salad.

window box

strawberry plants

potting compost (soil)

tomato plants

nasturtium seeds

lettuce seeds

radish seeds

1 Fill the window box with potting compost (soil) to just below the rim.

2 Plant the tomatoes in the back corners of the window box.

3 Plant the strawberries about 30 cm (12 in) away from the tomatoes.

4 Sow radish and lettuce seeds 1 cm (½ in) apart. The radishes will come first, then the lettuces can have the space.

5 Sow some nasturtium seeds in the corners so that they can grow up and trail over the edge. Water thoroughly.

Character Skittles

Plastic bottles make excellent skittles, especially if you paint them to look like people. You can play the game indoors as well as outside if you use a soft ball.

YOU WILL NEED
clean, empty plastic bottles
fretsaw
newspaper
PVA (white) glue and brush
water
paper baubles
strong glue
acrylic paint, in assorted colours
paintbrush
ribbon, in various colours and
    patterns

newspaper

brush

paper bauble

plastic bottle

PVA (white) glue

ribbon

paint

fretsaw

strong glue

1 Remove the labels from the bottles by soaking them in water. Saw off the top of each bottle as shown.

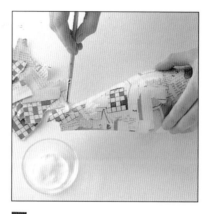

2 Cover the bottles in papier-mâché and leave to dry.

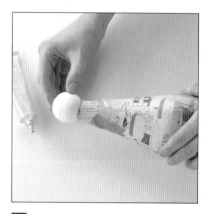

3 Glue a paper bauble on top of each bottle, using strong glue.

4 Paint the bottles and the bauble faces with a base coat. Leave the paint to dry.

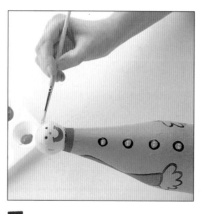

5 Give each skittle a different character by painting different coloured hair and clothes. Leave the second coat of paint to dry.

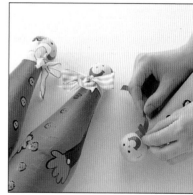

6 Tie a piece of ribbon in a bow round the neck of each skittle.

Big Foot Stilts

You will love walking about on these giant feet! If possible, ask the person for whom the stilts are intended to stand on the can so that you can measure the length of rope needed.

YOU WILL NEED
2 large, empty cans, the same
  size
softened plasticine
bradawl
spray paint
enamel paint, in contrasting
  colour
paintbrush
sticky stars
rope, see above for
  measurement

sticky stars

spray paint

enamel paint

paintbrush

cans

rope

bradawl

plasticine

1 Remove the labels from the cans. Place a ball of softened plasticine on either side of the top of each can. Pierce a hole through the plasticine with a bradawl then remove the plasticine.

2 Place the cans on a well-protected surface, preferably outdoors. Spray with spray paint and leave to dry. Spray on a second coat if necessary.

3 Paint the top of the cans with enamel paint. Leave to dry.

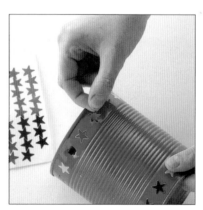

4 Decorate the cans with sticky stars.

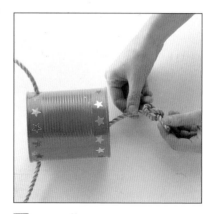

5 Ask the child to stand on the cans. Measure the length of rope needed then thread one piece of rope through the holes on each can. Tie the ends in a knot.

6 Burn the ends of rope to prevent them from fraying.

Soaring Kite

Take this kite out on a windy day and you will be able to play for hours. Choose a bright colour for the tail, to contrast with the kite and show up against the sky.

YOU WILL NEED

50 cm x 70 cm (20 in x 27½ in) lightweight fabric
ruler
pencil
scissors
sewing thread
needle
65 cm (26 in) thin, strong nylon thread
small piece of contrast fabric, for the tail
2 pieces of 5 mm (³⁄₁₆ in) dowel, 68 cm (26¾ in) and 48 cm (19 in) long

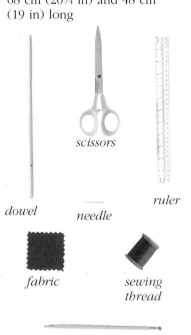

scissors

ruler

dowel   *needle*

fabric   *sewing thread*

pencil

1 Fold the fabric in half lengthways. On the raw edges, mark 25 cm (10 in) down from the top. Cut from the fold point at each end to this mark. Open out the kite shape, fold over, place the cut edges together and stitch the seam.

2 Stitch the nylon thread securely to the two corners on either side of the kite.

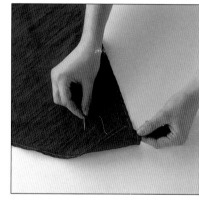

3 Fold in each corner about 1 cm (½ in). Secure with two tacking stitches about 1 cm (½ in) apart, to go either side of the dowel.

4 Cut a strip of fabric for the tail and stitch on to the bottom of the kite.

5 Lay the two pieces of dowel across the kite and insert the ends into the pockets made by the tacking stitches.

The sun is shining, you're on holiday and it's summer time! There's nothing better than to be outdoors at this time of year. Nature is at its most beautiful, and if you planted seeds in the spring you will see that the flowers are now in bloom and smelling sweet – watch the bees buzz about as they collect their pollen. If you visit the seaside, look closely in the rock pools and along the beach and see what treasures you can find – you might even be able to take some objects home as souvenirs.

summer

How Tall is a Tree?

Field guides and other books often tell us the height of a tree. But how do we actually measure it?

YOU WILL NEED
pencil
stick
tape measure or ruler
notebook

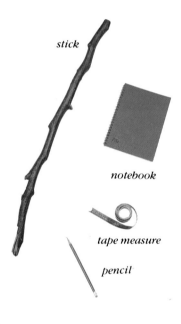

stick

notebook

tape measure

pencil

1 Stand in front of the tree. Hold out a pencil at arm's length so that you can see it and the tree at the same time. Ask a friend to stand at the bottom of the tree.

2 Line the pencil up so that the top of it is in line with the top of the tree. Move your thumb down the pencil until it is level with the bottom of the tree.

3 Turn the pencil so that it is horizontal, still keeping your thumb level with the bottom of the tree. Ask your friend to walk away from the trunk. Call and tell her to stop when she is level with the top of the pencil.

4 Mark the place where your friend is standing with a stick. Measure the distance from the stick to the tree. This distance is the same as the height of the tree. Record your findings in your notebook.

How Big and How Old is a Tree?

Some trees are very old. We can measure how big and old a tree is very easily.

YOU WILL NEED
rope
tape measure or ruler
notebook
pencil

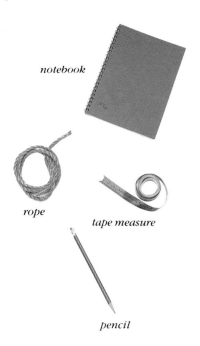

notebook

rope

tape measure

pencil

1 How big is a tree? Take a piece of rope to measure the tree trunk. Put it around the tree and keep your finger on the place where the rope overlaps. A large oak tree like this one could be several hundred years old.

NATURE TIP
Next time you go for a walk look at the trees. How many really old trees can you find? These will be the tallest and/or those with the thickest trunks.

2 Lay the rope out straight on the ground and measure to the place you have marked with your finger. This will equal the distance around the outside of the trunk (the girth).

3 How old is a tree? The tree rings on a log can tell us its age. The tree grows a new ring every year.

4 Count the rings and you will discover the age of the log. If the tree has one hundred and fifty rings then the log is one hundred and fifty years old. Record your findings in your notebook with a pencil.

Turn Detective

Watch out! Be careful where you step. There is a fascinating, hidden world going on unnoticed right beneath your feet. Take time to look and you will be amazed what there is to discover on a mini safari in a garden.

YOU WILL NEED
string
2 bamboo canes or sticks
magnifying glass
notebook and pencil

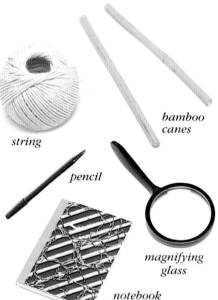

string

bamboo canes

pencil

magnifying glass

notebook

1 Tie a piece of string about 1.5 m (5 ft) long to 2 bamboo canes or sticks.

2 Peg this down across some long grass or a woodland edge.

3 Creep along the line of string very slowly, centimetre by centimetre, (inch by inch) with your nose to the ground looking through a magnifying glass.

4 Try to identify what you find with the help of nature books, or start a nature diary to make notes in.

Garden with a Buzz

To encourage beautiful butterflies and buzzing bees into your garden, grow a few of their favourite plants to tempt them in from miles around. Many butterflies are now becoming scarce, so every butterfly-friendly plant that you can grow will help them to survive. Bees and butterflies like lots of sunshine so put your buzzy garden in a sunny spot.

YOU WILL NEED
pebbles
a large planter or half barrel
potting compost (soil) or equal
  quantities of garden soil and
  potting compost (soil)
a selection of suitable plants such as
  phlox, aster, lavender, angel's
  pincushion, verbena, blue lobelia
trowel

half barrel

plants

pebbles

*potting compost
and soil*

trowel

1 Put a few pebbles in the bottom of the barrel or planter for drainage, then fill with compost or an equal mixture of soil and compost.

2 Plant phlox and aster in the middle because they are tallest.

3 Plant lavender, angel's pincushion and verbena around the edge.

DID YOU KNOW?
As bees collect their food, they also do the very important job of pollinating the flower, and so provide us with fruit, like apples and pears.

4 Plant blue lobelia in the front, so it tumbles over the edge. Water the tub.

GARDENER'S TIP
Other friendly plants are: broom, catmint, delphiniums, nasturtiums, oxeye daisy, petunias, primroses, stocks, sweet williams and thrift.

Making a Keep Net

This keep net is a safe way to watch butterflies for a short time without hurting them.

YOU WILL NEED
netting or gauze
scissors
needle and thread
4 bamboo canes
butterfly or fishing net
notebook
pencil

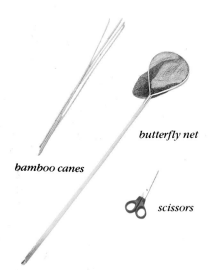

butterfly net

bamboo canes

scissors

netting

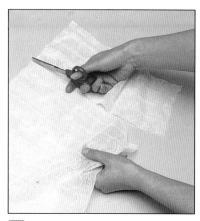

1 Cut a square piece of netting 30 cm × 30 cm (12 in × 12 in) and a rectangle of netting 120 cm × 50 cm (48 in × 20 in).

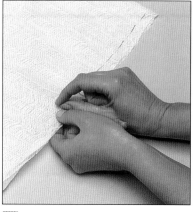

2 Fold the rectangle in half. Sew the long sides together.

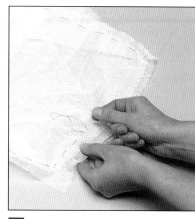

3 Sew the square top onto one end.

4 Push four garden canes into the ground in a square, each 30 cm (12 in) apart. Drape the net over the top.

5 Carefully catch a butterfly with a butterfly or fishing net and gently put it into the net. Try not to touch the butterflies' wings or you could injure them.

6 Look through the net to identify your butterfly. This one is a small tortoiseshell. Draw it and make notes in your notebook. Release the butterfly afterwards.

NATURE TIP

Butterflies drink sugary nectar from flowers. Plant these flowers in your garden and the butterflies will come to feed from them: buddleia, lavender, golden rod, iceplant, hyssop, asclepias (milkweed) and honeysuckle. Cabbages, nasturtiums and stinging nettles also attract butterflies. They lay their eggs on these plants.

Making a Light Trap for Moths

Moths and other insects fly at night. They are attracted to the bright lights of electric lightbulbs. You can study them using this simple piece of equipment.

YOU WILL NEED
large, thick plastic bottle (the type used for household cleaning liquids)
scissors
sticky tape
desk lamp
small collecting pots
paintbrush
field guide
notebook
pencil

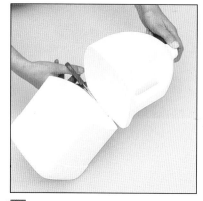

! **1** Ask an adult to clean the bottle, and cut the top off to make a funnel.

2 Stand the top upside down in the base of the bottle. Tape the two together.

desk lamp
collecting pot

scissors
sticky tape

plastic bottle

paintbrush

3 Take the light trap outside. Place a desk lamp so that it shines over the top of the funnel. You may need to stand the lamp on a brick if it is too short.

! **4** Ask an adult to plug the lamp into the nearest electricity socket. DO NOT USE IN WET WEATHER. At night, turn the lamp on and leave the light shining for several hours.

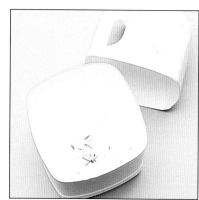

5 Moths fly into the light and fall down into the funnel. They are then trapped in the bottom section. Remove the funnel and see which moths and other flying insects have been caught in the bottom of the bottle.

6 Put the moths and insects into small collecting pots, using a small paintbrush to pick them up gently. Identify them with a field guide, and make notes and drawings about them in your nature notebook. Carefully release the moths and insects afterwards.

Making a Fishing Net

This net is a useful piece of equipment which is easy to make. Use it to catch flying insects, or for pond dipping and rock pooling.

YOU WILL NEED
rectangle of netting, 90 cm × 30 cm
   (36 in × 12 in)
needle and thread
wire coathanger
scissors or pliers
bamboo cane
jubilee clip or wire

netting

pliers

bamboo cane

wire coathanger

jubilee clip

thread

scissors

1 Fold the piece of netting in half and stitch along the side and the bottom.

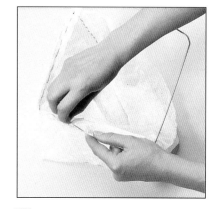

2 Open the coathanger so that it makes a square or round shape.

3 Fold the top of the net over the wire and stitch it in place.

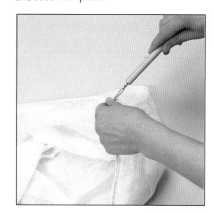

5 Carefully push the wires into the end of the cane. (You may need an adult's help.)

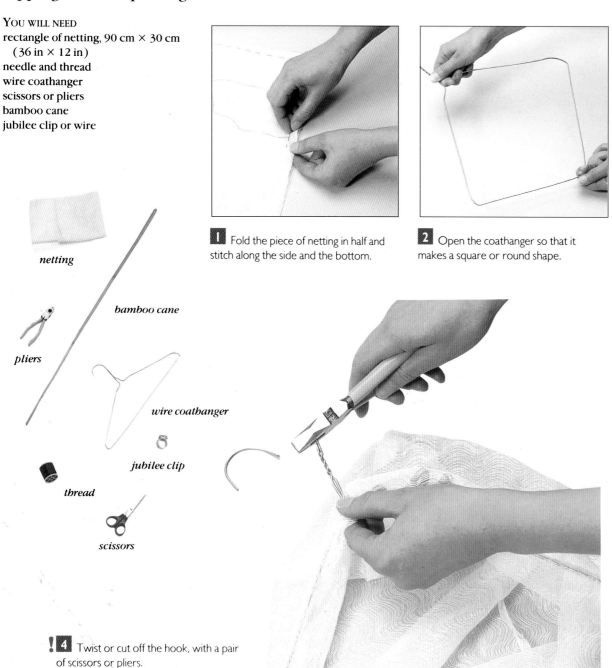

! 4 Twist or cut off the hook, with a pair of scissors or pliers.

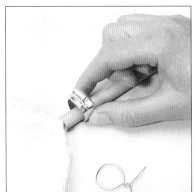

6 Secure the net to the cane with a jubilee clip or a piece of wire tightly twisted around the top. This will stop the net falling off if you get it caught up in pond weeds.

Rock Pools

Many animals such as shrimps, crabs and baby fish live in rock pools. Here they find a safe place to wait until the tide comes in again.

YOU WILL NEED
fishing net
bucket
plastic bags
notebook
pencil

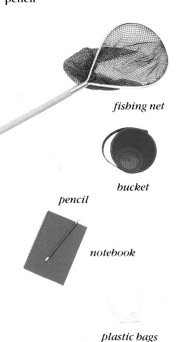

fishing net

bucket

pencil

notebook

plastic bags

! SAFETY TIP

Take care on slippery rocks. Do not get cut off by incoming tides.

1 When the tide goes out, animals on the beach must close up or hide and wait until the water returns. In the rock pool however, the animals can continue to swim and feed.

2 Some animals such as limpets and anemones attach themselves to rocks. They can move, but only very slowly.

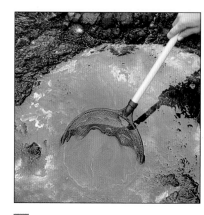

3 Sweep a fishing net through the sandy bottom of the pool. You may catch shrimps, crabs and tiny fish that lie buried in the sand.

! 4 Be careful if you find a crab. Do not handle it roughly because you may damage its legs. You can pick it up safely by holding it across the back of its shell. This way it cannot nip you!

5 Lift up rocks carefully. Many animals live underneath them. Always replace rocks gently so that you do not damage the microhabitat and the animals underneath.

6 Collect animals in a bucket or plastic bag. Identify them and make notes in your notebook. In this bucket there are hermit crabs, shore crabs, periwinkles and a sea anemone. Do not forget to release them into the water afterwards.

Beachcombing at the Seaside

We all like to go to the seaside. Be a nature detective on the beach and see what treasures you can find.

YOU WILL NEED
bucket
plastic bags
notebook
pencil

pencil

notebook

plastic bags

bucket

1 Look for animals under seaweed and rocks where they stay nice and damp. Cuttlefish, crab and urchin shells, feathers and other animals are often washed up. You will find them at the highest place reached by the tide, known as the strandline.

2 You will find a variety of shells all over the beach.

3 Look for unusual stones and pebble sculptures, fossils and minerals. The holes in this large stone were drilled by rock-boring clams. Can you see the Indian's head? This is a real stone that was just picked up on a beach.

4 Who lives under the sand? Look for worm holes and dig down to find the worm beneath. Collect animals and shells and put them in a bucket or plastic bags. Make notes in your notebook, and release living creatures afterwards.

! 5 A lot of garbage is washed up onto the beach. Ropes, plastic and driftwood are harmless, but fishing tackle, bottles and canisters can be dangerous. Take care and do not touch. Some can contain dangerous chemicals.

Beach Art

You can never get bored on a beach. Draw pictures in the sand or create these masterpieces.

1 Collect shells on the beach and arrange them to make a picture.

2 Decorate your picture with seaweed, stones, feathers and driftwood – in fact anything that you can find.

5 This face is made from seaweed and stones.

NATURE TIP

You could take a picture of your beach art so you can remember it after it has been washed away.

3 This driftwood ship has a stone cabin and funnel. The smoke and sea are made of seaweed. The sand below is rippled and looks like waves.

4 Different shaped seaweeds look like trees and plants in a garden.

Seaweed Pictures

Making seaweed pictures was a popular pastime during Victorian times, 100 years ago.

YOU WILL NEED
shallow dish or tray
card (cardboard)
scissors
pieces of thin seaweed (collect as
　many different colours as you can)
paper towels
newspapers

shallow dish

paper towel

*card
(cardboard)*

scissors

seaweed

1 Fill the dish with water. Soak a piece of card (cardboard) in it.

2 Use the scissors to cut off a small piece of seaweed. Float the seaweed on top of the piece of card. Spread out the frond with your fingers by letting it float and fan out into the water.

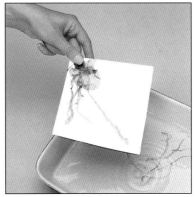

3 Slowly lift out the card and gently pour off the water. Hold onto the seaweed with your thumb as you pour.

4 Repeat with more weed and drain. Blot with paper towel and leave to dry on the card. If the picture becomes crinkly when it dries, simply soak it again. Press lightly under a pile of newspapers and leave to dry.

Collecting Shells

Sea shells are found and collected on beaches all over the world. You can quickly build up a beautiful collection of shells that will look great displayed in a box or as a picture on the wall.

YOU WILL NEED
bucket
field guide
notebook
pencil
clear varnish
paintbrush
coloured or white card (cardboard)
PVA (white) glue

bucket

clear varnish

PVA (white) glue

card (cardboard)

1 Collect empty, dead shells from the beach into a bucket.

2 Wash them thoroughly in fresh water at home. Leave them outside in the sun to dry for several days. If you do not do this they will become smelly.

3 Use a field guide to identify your shells. Make notes and drawings about them in your nature notebook.

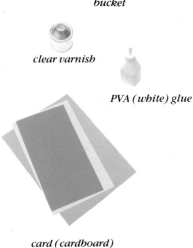

4 Select the best specimen of each shell and paint them with clear varnish.

NATURE NOTE

Some shells are protected and should not be removed from the beach. Be sure to follow local guidelines before taking them.

5 Stick them onto card (cardboard). You can keep the cards with your collection in a box or frame them and hang them on the wall.

A Watery World

No garden is complete without the sight and sound of water. Great for toe-dipping on a hot, sunny day, this mini-pond is too small for fish but a welcome watering spot for thirsty birds. Any large container can be used to make a mini-pond, as long as it is watertight! A washing-up (dish washing) bowl is a bit too shallow but would do at a pinch. A toy-tidy, like this one which is deeper, is ideal. So give away some toys and splash in some water instead.

You WILL NEED
large, wide container
gravel
2 aquatic plants like golden sedge
 and monkey flower
lead from a wine bottle top
strands of oxygenating weed
flower pot
potting compost (soil)
small floating plants

container

aquatic plants

gravel

floating plants

flower pot

oxygenating weed

lead

1 Find a large, wide container and put a layer of gravel in the bottom.

2 Fill the container up with water almost to the top.

3 Lower the aquatic plants (which should already be in net pots when you buy them) gently into the water around the edge of the container.

4 Attach a piece of lead from a wine bottle top round the base of pieces of oxygenating weed to weigh them down.

5 Pot the bunch into an ordinary (regular) flower pot and put a layer of gravel on the surface.

6 Sink the pot into the mini-pond, then add a few floaters like water lettuce and floating ferns. Plant your pond in a hole in the garden so that it keeps cool.

Time Capsules

Seeds are amazing things – tiny packages that are ready to spring into life when you add water and soil. They are also full of surprises, you could discover a completely new flower from seed you have collected yourself.

DID YOU KNOW?
Most seeds last for a few years, some even last for about 50! Store in envelopes in a cool, dry place over the winter until the spring, or whenever you want to sow them.

YOU WILL NEED
paper bag
newspaper
seed tray
sheet of paper
envelopes
pen

paper bag

newspaper

seed tray

envelopes

pen

paper

1 Only collect seeds on a dry, sunny day and use a paper bag rather than a plastic one to put them in.

2 Put a layer of newspaper in a seed tray and spread out the collected seeds on top. Put them in a dry, warm place for a couple of days to dry thoroughly.

3 Fold a sheet of paper in half, then open out flat so there is just a crease. Rub the seed capsules between your fingers to try and get just the seeds out.

4 Carefully pick out all the bits of stem and seed pods. Blowing lightly can help to remove some of the lighter rubbish.

5 Pour the clean seeds into small envelopes (they should collect in the paper crease which makes it easier to pour them into the envelopes).

6 Don't forget to write the names of the plants on the envelopes – or you will never remember what the seeds are.

Desert Garden

If you like dreaming of hot, sunny places and plants that are not too much trouble, then cacti and succulents are the plants for you. Keep this desert garden on a sunny windowsill and water it well during the summer but hardly at all in the winter. With this winter rest, a cactus might surprise you with a dazzling display of flowers.

YOU WILL NEED
clay flower pot
pebbles
special cacti compost (soil) or
 potting compost (soil), grit and
sand
rocks
cacti and succulent plants
strips of folded newspaper
gravel

potting compost (soil)

cacti and succulent plants

newspaper

grit and sand

rocks

flower pot

pebbles

1 Find a container that is not too deep but quite wide at the top – it must have holes for drainage. Put a handful of pebbles in the bottom. Fill the pot with special cacti compost (soil) or mix your own, using equal quantities of potting compost (soil), grit and sand.

2 Position one or two large rocks in the container.

3 Pick the cacti up with strips of folded newspaper to protect yourself from getting pricked, and plant them around the rocks.

4 Cover the surface with gravel. During the spring and summer water like ordinary houseplants, but during the winter water about once a month when the compost (soil) is very dry.

A Wild One

Native plants are those that have grown naturally in the countryside for thousands of years. Some of the most colourful ones are cornfield flowers, but many are quite rare now. To enjoy them this summer, grow a pot full of wild flowers to stand on your doorstep.

YOU WILL NEED
pebbles
very large flower pot
garden soil
packet of wild flower seeds

flower pot

garden soil

pebbles

wild flower seeds

1 Put a few pebbles in the bottom of the pot for drainage.

GARDENER'S TIP
Don't forget to keep watering as the flowers grow! Pots need much more watering than beds because the water drains away.

2 Fill the pot with garden soil, taking out any bits of roots or large stones.

3 Make sure the surface is level, then sprinkle a large pinch of flower seeds evenly on top.

4 Cover the seeds lightly with soil, just so you can't see them any more, and water them in with a gentle sprinkle.

Scare them off!

Fed up with those pesky pigeons stealing your precious plants? Give them a fright by making a scarecrow out of odds and ends that you find lying around. Model it on someone you know and give them a shock too! My dog would not stop barking at this one, so it certainly works!

YOU WILL NEED
2 sticks – one 1.85 m (6 ft) long, the other 1.25 m (4 ft) long
nails
hammer
spade
old pillowcase
permanent marking pen
stuffing: straw, newspapers in plastic bags
thick string
safety pins
old clothes

pillowcase   *hat*

scarf

shirt   *straw stuffing*

⚠ SAFETY NOTE
Always take great care when using a hammer.

1 Put the longer stick on the ground and lay the shorter one across it about 30 cm (12 in) from the top. Nail them together with a couple of nails so that the frame is good and strong. Dig a 30 cm (12 in) hole, plant the frame and fill up the hole with soil.

2 Draw a face on the pillowcase with the open end down. Then bring the top corners together and tie. Fill the pillowcase with stuffing.

3 Put the head over the top of the frame so that the stick goes up into the stuffing. Tie the open end of the pillowcase tightly around the stick with a piece of string. Pin the hat to the head.

4 Tie the trouser bottoms up and fill them with stuffing.

5 Attach the trousers to the frame by running string through the back belt loop and around the stick.

6 Put the shirt on so the ends of the short stick go through the armholes and fill it with stuffing. Now you have a permanent guest in your garden!

Terrific Tyres

Old tyres get a new and completely different lease of life with a lick of paint. They make perfect containers for growing all sorts of plants and are ideal for a first garden.

YOU WILL NEED
coloured emulsion (acrylic) paints
paintbrush
2 tyres
potting compost (soil) and
 garden soil
selection of bedding plants

tyre

paint

paintbrush

potting compost and garden soil

bedding plants

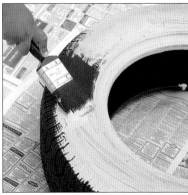

1 Use ordinary emulsion (acrylic) to paint the tyres – any colours look good, the brighter the better.

2 Put one tyre on top of another. Two is deep enough, three would be better for larger plants.

3 Fill them up with potting compost (soil), or equal quantities of garden soil and compost. It takes rather a lot to fill the tyres, so to cut down on the amount, stuff newspaper into the tyres.

4 Put the tallest plants in first – this is a cosmea (cosmos).

5 Surround with smaller plants like geraniums, pansies and marigolds.

GARDENER'S TIP
You can get old tyres for free at most garages. For something cheap and fast-growing, try pumpkin plants. A ring of lobelia will grow happily if planted between the two tyres.

6 Plant some delicate trailing plants to grow over the edge. Start your tyre garden off well by giving it a lot of water. Keep watering through the summer and don't let it get too dry.

Miniature Garden

Even without a garden you can become a great garden designer and make the perfect landscape – only in miniature. It is a lot less work than the real thing and just as much fun.

YOU WILL NEED
deep seed tray or wooden box
potting compost (soil)
foil pie dish
small stones
twigs
raffia
ivy
alpine plants
moss
grit
model garden furniture
plant cuttings
dried flowers

potting compost (soil)

moss

stones   *grit*

seed tray

foil pie dish

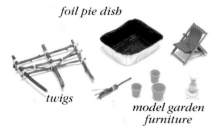

twigs   *model garden furniture*

1 Fill a seed tray with potting compost, (soil) then start putting in the most permanent features. A foil pie dish makes a great pond and a rockery is easy to make from small stones.

2 Make natural looking fences and trellises from dead twigs, tied together with raffia. Some little pieces of ivy stem look good growing on the fence, it might even take root.

3 Alpine plants are worth investing in if you can. They are perfect because they stay quite small.

5 Use grit to make paths and patios.

4 Use some moss to lay a luxurious lawn. You can find it growing outside in cool, damp places, or you can try growing it yourself by sprinkling a handful of dried moss on the watered surface of a little seed tray.

GARDENER'S TIP

To help the miniature garden to last as long as possible, choose a deep seed tray, a gravel tray or even a strong wooden box. An ordinary (regular) seed tray is fine to start with, but because they are so shallow, the garden will only last for a few weeks.

Keep your miniature garden inside on a cool windowsill or, even better, outside in a sheltered corner and make sure that you keep it watered, at least every day in the summer. These are just some ideas – don't forget the swing, the compost bin, the vegetable patch and the greenhouse made from half a plastic bottle!

6 Add whatever bits and pieces you can find at home to make an assortment of garden furniture and decorations. Finally, fill up the flower beds with dried flowers and little cuttings from any interesting bushes (better ask first).

Grow Spaghetti

Yes, it's true! This type of marrow (summer squash) is packed with vegetable spaghetti. It only needs cooking to spill out its treasures. Bake it in the oven, or boil it until soft, add some butter and give it a twirl.

YOU WILL NEED
small flower pot
potting compost (soil)
spaghetti marrow seeds
hand fork
manure or garden compost
trowel
hand fork

flower pots

spaghetti marrow seeds

potting compost (soil)

DID YOU KNOW?
All marrows (squashes) have separate male and female flowers and to get fruit they need to be pollinated. It is easy to tell which flower is which because the female one always has a swelling at the bottom beneath the petals.

1 Fill a small flower pot with potting compost (soil) and make it level. Plant 3 seeds, pushing them in about 1 cm (½ in) deep.

2 Prepare the soil well, by forking over and adding some manure or garden compost.

3 When the young plant has 3 or 4 fully grown leaves and the weather is nice and warm, plant it outside in the prepared spot.

4 When the plant flowers, play the part of a bee by picking off a male flower and dusting the yellow pollen onto the middle of the female one to pollinate it.

5 They are very greedy plants for both water and food. When the first flowers appear, start to add some fertilizer to its water once a week. Choose a fertilizer made especially for flowers and fruit and you will be rewarded with plates piled with vegetable spaghetti.

Scrumptious Strawberries

Summer just wouldn't be the same without a bowl of freshly picked, ripe-red, juicy strawberries, lightly sprinkled with sugar and served with ice-cream. They are surprisingly quick and easy to grow and, providing you look after them, you will get free pick-your-own for years to come. A strawberry plant grows several long stems which have baby plants along them. These are called runners and can be potted up to produce plants that will have fruit next year.

1 Fill a small flower pot to the top with garden soil.

2 Choose a long, healthy stem that has a baby strawberry plant starting to grow somewhere along its length. Cut off the stem beyond the baby plant.

YOU WILL NEED
small flower pot
trowel
strawberry plant
secateurs (clippers)
tent peg

secateurs (clippers)

tent peg

flower pot

3 Position the baby plant in the pot of soil and pin it in place using a tent peg.

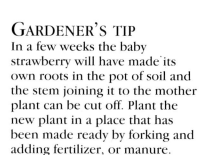

4 Push the tent peg out through one of the holes in the bottom of the pot. Then position the pot next to the mother plant and push the peg in to secure it.

GARDENER'S TIP

In a few weeks the baby strawberry will have made its own roots in the pot of soil and the stem joining it to the mother plant can be cut off. Plant the new plant in a place that has been made ready by forking and adding fertilizer, or manure.

Minty Tea

Sprigs of mint look and taste great in cool summer drinks and mint tea is delicious either hot or cold at any time of the year.

YOU WILL NEED
mint leaves
teapot
boiling water
sugar or honey to taste

mint leaves

teapot

! SAFETY NOTE
Always take great care when pouring boiling water.

1 Pick a large handful of mint leaves.

2 Tear the leaves into little pieces.

3 Put the leaves into the teapot.

4 Pour on boiling water and leave to steep for 5 minutes before pouring out to drink immediately, or leave until cool and then chill in the refrigerator. Add a little sugar or honey for a special treat.

GARDENER'S TIP
Mint grows very quickly by long running stems that creep through the soil making new plants along their length. Cut one of these off and plant it in a large pot.

Pots of Herbs

A handful of herbs adds the finishing touch to all sorts of dishes. You can keep this pot anywhere in the garden, on a balcony or even on a window sill, to give you lovely, fresh snippets just when you want them. I have put in a silver and a golden thyme because thyme is one of the best herbs for pots, not growing too large and great for soups and sauces.

YOU WILL NEED
large pot
pebbles
potting compost (soil)
selection of herbs such as curry
 plant, marjoram, parsley, chives
 and thyme

herbs   *large pot*

potting compost (soil)   *pebbles*

1 Put a good handful of pebbles in the bottom of the pot so water can drain out easily (herbs don't like soggy feet).

GARDENER'S TIP
Larger herbs like mint, rosemary and fennel, are great for the first year, but in the second they will outgrow the pot and swamp anything else in it, so it is really best to give them a pot each. Remember to keep all your herbs well watered but not too soggy.

2 Fill the pot almost full with potting compost (soil). The curry plant is the tallest, so plant that in the middle.

3 Plant the marjoram towards the back because it is the next biggest.

4 Work around the pot planting chives, parsley and thyme. You can start using the herbs as soon as you like!

Long-lasting Lavender

Need something to make your room smell nice? Well, I've got just the thing – some good old-fashioned English lavender. Fill bowls with dried lavender or make into muslin (cheesecloth) bags to put among your clothes.

YOU WILL NEED
scissors
fresh lavender
raffia
sheet of paper
small bowl

scissors

raffia

paper

bowl

lavender

1 Cut whole stalks of lavender when the flowers are showing colour, but are not fully opened.

2 Tie them in small, loose bundles with a bit of raffia.

3 Hang them upside down in a warm, dry place for a few days.

4 When the flowers are completely dry, rub them free of the stalks on to a sheet of paper. You can use the lavender to scent rooms or clothes.

! SAFETY NOTE
Always take great care when using any sharp objects.

Pressed Flowers

Pressing flowers is an excellent way to preserve and keep them. Some specimens in museums are hundreds of years old. You can use pressed flowers to make pictures, or to decorate many different things.

YOU WILL NEED
fresh flowers
tissues or paper towels
flowerpress or book
PVA (white) glue
paper or card (cardboard)

PVA (white) glue

fresh flowers

flowerpress

1 Pick a selection of different flowers.

2 You should not pick wildflowers unless they are weeds growing on private land – and you have the permission of the land-owner.

3 Arrange the flowers on a tissue or a paper towel in a flowerpress or between the pages of a book. If you use a book, make sure that the juice from the flowers will not stain the pages.

4 Spread the petals, and cover them with a second sheet of tissue or paper towel. Replace the top of the flowerpress or close the book. Tighten the bolts on the flowerpress, or, place some more books on top of the book containing the flowers. Leave in a warm, dry place for at least two weeks. Do not peek too soon, or the flowers will not dry properly.

5 When the flowers are dry, carefully lift the dried flowers, and stick them onto paper or card (cardboard) with PVA (white) glue. Use them to decorate greetings cards, writing paper, pictures and lampshades, in fact almost anything you can think of.

Potpourri

Potpourri has been used for centuries to make rooms and stored linen smell nice and fresh.

YOU WILL NEED
fresh flowers
fresh herbs, such as lavender and
    rosemary
scissors
string
foil dish or tray
bowl
spices, such as nutmeg, cinnamon
    sticks and cloves (optional)
airtight jars or bags

lavender

fresh flowers

cinnamon sticks

fresh herbs

foil dish

string

scissors

1 Pick the flowers and herbs. This plant is lavender.

2 Cut the herbs and tie them into bunches. This plant is rosemary.

3 Hang the bunches of herbs up in a warm place to dry.

4 Put fresh rose petals, small flowers, flower buds, herb leaves and herb flowers onto a foil dish or tray. Put them somewhere warm such as an airing cupboard or near a radiator to dry.

5 When the herbs and flowers are completely dry, strip the leaves from the herb bunches. Put them into a bowl with the dried petals and flowerheads.

6 Add the spices (if using) and mix well. If you wish, you can also add a few drops of perfumed oil. Mix well. Store in airtight jars or bags. To use, place in a shallow dish or basket so that the scent of the flowers, herbs and spices can escape into the air.

At the end of summer, nature starts to prepare itself for the coming winter, but this doesn't mean you'll be short of things to look out for! Everybody knows that trees lose their leaves in autumn (fall), but have you ever collected fallen leaves and made rubbings of their patterns to make pictures for your bedroom wall? Now that the trees have no leaves you can get a much better look at them; even better, why not try to grow a tree yourself?

autumn

Parts of a Tree

Trees are the giants of the plant world. See if you can find these different parts of a tree.

2 **Twigs:** In winter, twigs and branches can help you to identify a tree. From the top, these twigs are: birch, ash, apple, oak and willow.

3 **Trunk bark and roots:** We do not often see a tree's roots. These willow trees are growing by a pond. Can you see the fine, hairy rootlets?

1 **Leaves:** These come in many shapes and sizes. Some have toothed edges. Others are divided up into many smaller leaflets. Pine leaves are like needles.

4 **Flowers:** Some trees have flowers with petals. But many have green or yellow catkins and do not look like flowers at all.

5 **Fruit:** There is a great variety of tree fruits and seeds. Fruit and nuts are spread by animals who try to eat them. Other seeds have wings that spin through the air like helicopters.

6 **Cones:** Pines are usually evergreen. Most do not lose their leaves in winter. Their leaves are like needles. Their fruit are seeds which are carried in pine cones.

7 Deciduous trees like the walnut opposite lose their leaves in winter. Every autumn the green leaves change colour to yellow, brown or red. They shrivel and fall from the tree. Can you see them on the ground?

Celebration Tree

There is something very special about planting a tree. It will live longer than us and grow much taller, so what better way to celebrate a new baby, a birthday or a family reunion? Trees are extremely important because they create the air that all living things breathe. Not everyone has room in their garden for a majestic oak or beech tree, but you could plant a smaller species such as a Whitebeam. This little tree has silvery, white undersides to the leaves and beautiful, scented white flowers followed by bright red fruits.

YOU WILL NEED
spade
sheet of plastic
fork
manure or garden compost
small tree
stake
hammer
2 tree ties

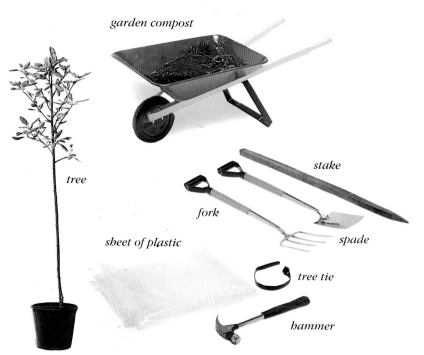

garden compost

tree

fork

stake

spade

sheet of plastic

tree tie

hammer

1 Remove the turf and dig a hole at least 7.5 cm (3 in) deeper than the depth of the pot which the tree is in, putting all the soil onto a sheet of plastic to keep the garden tidy.

2 Fork over the bottom of the hole and add a generous helping of manure or compost. This helps to feed the tree and will also help to hold water in the soil under its roots.

3 Take the tree out of its pot carefully and place it in position.

4 Put the stake in the hole close to the roots and hammer in place. The stake should be just below the first branch.

! SAFETY NOTE
Always take great care when using any sharp objects.

GARDENER'S TIP
If you cannot get special tree ties, use a pair of old tights (panty hose) instead, to stop the tree rubbing against the stake.

5 Start to put the soil back in the planting hole, firming it lightly and gently around the tree roots.

6 Fix two tree ties on securely, one at the bottom and one at the top of the stake. Finally, give it a really good drink to set it off on a long and healthy life.

GARDENER'S TIP
After about 3 years, when the tree is well established, the stake can be removed carefully.

Life in a Tree

Many animals make their homes among the leaves and branches of a tree. Beat a branch and discover the insects that live in the jungle world of the leaves.

YOU WILL NEED
large roll of white paper or cloth
stick
small paintbrush
collecting pots
lenses or bug box
field guide
notebook
pencil

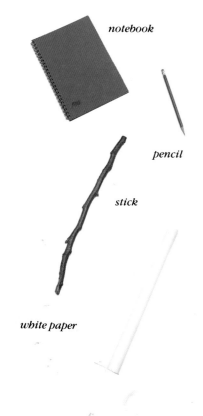

notebook

pencil

stick

white paper

collecting pot

1 Spread the paper or cloth under a large branch.

2 Shake the branch over the paper or cloth and beat it with a stick. Do not beat it too hard or you will crack the wood.

3 The insects will fall down onto the paper or cloth. Pick them up with the paintbrush and put them into the collecting pots.

4 Use lenses, a bug box, and a field guide to identify your specimens. In your notebook, write a list of everything that you have found. How many of each species are there? Make pencil drawings of them.

5 Release your captive insects, preferably under the tree that you found them in, or, at least somewhere safe. Now try beating a branch from a different type of tree. Which has the most insects living among its leaves?

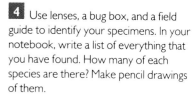

Nature Detective

Whenever you are out near trees, look for clues to the animals that live there. Keep your eyes and ears open. Be a nature detective!

YOU WILL NEED
notebook
pencil
plastic bags
collecting box or pot

collecting box

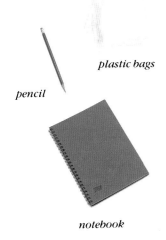

pencil

plastic bags

notebook

1 Look for signs of feeding such as pine cones, nuts and fruit gnawed by squirrels, mice and other animals. Collect these specimens and record them in your notebook.

2 Look for nest holes. This hole goes down inside a hollow tree. It is being used by a fox. Look up into the branches of the tree and you may see woodpeckers' and other birds' nest holes.

3 Look for insect holes. Many insects and their larvae burrow into wood. These tunnels were made by bark beetles.

4 Look for rotten wood. Woodpeckers drill holes in rotten wood to look for burrowing insects. Other animals scratch at the wood to get at the insects inside.

Bark and Leaf Rubbing

Feel the ridges and veins on a leaf. By rubbing with a crayon you can use these ridges to make some beautiful copies of the leaves that you find.

YOU WILL NEED
paper
wax crayons or a soft pencil
folder
scrapbook
sticky tape or PVA (white) glue

folder

wax crayons

paper

1 For a bark rubbing, put a piece of paper against a tree trunk. Hold it firmly so that it does not move.

2 Rub the paper all over with a wax crayon or a soft pencil. The pattern of the bark will appear on the paper. Now try another tree. Different trees have different patterns of bark.

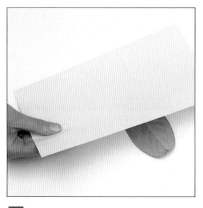

3 For a leaf rubbing, put a leaf on a smooth surface like a table. Cover with a piece of paper.

4 Hold the paper down firmly. Gently rub over the leaf with a wax crayon or soft pencil. You can store your finished rubbings in a folder or stick them into a scrapbook.

Collecting Spiders' Webs

Garden or orb-web spiders make beautiful webs that can be collected. This works best if you collect the webs on a wet, misty morning when they are covered with dew.

YOU WILL NEED
dark coloured card (cardboard) or
   paper
ozone-friendly hairspray
talcum powder
scissors

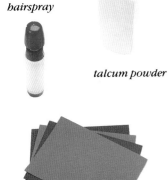

hairspray

talcum powder

*dark coloured card
(cardboard)*

scissors

! SAFETY NOTE
Always make sure the web is empty before you take it. Some spiders can give a very nasty bite, or are even poisonous.

1 Find a web in a hedge, on a fence, or on a building. Choose one with enough space to easily slide a piece of card (cardboard) or paper behind it.

2 Spray the web with hairspray.

3 Shake talcum powder over the web. Then spray with hairspray again.

4 Slide the card or paper behind the web and lift it up so that the web is caught on the card. Cut the threads which attach the web. Leave the mounted webs to dry. If you do not smudge them they will stay like this for quite some time.

Who Lives Under Logs and Stones?

Many small creatures live in the soil and in the dark and damp places that they find under logs, rocks and stones.

YOU WILL NEED
paintbrush or tweezers
collecting box
notebook
pencil
field guide

collecting box

paintbrush

notebook

pencil

NATURE TIP

It's fun to study small creatures, but remember always to take them back to their natural habitat.

1 Find a brick, stone, rock, or a log to look under. You can also look under planks of wood and other garden rubbish.

2 Lift the object up gently to see if anything is living underneath. Gently pick up the creatures with a paintbrush or tweezers.

3 Put any animals that you find into the collecting box. Gently roll the log or rock back afterwards to stop the microhabitat underneath from drying out. Make notes, draw, and use a field guide to identify the animals you have found.

4 You may be lucky enough to find some larger animals such as frogs, toads or newts (salamanders). When you have made notes, take the animals back where you found them, and replace them gently.

A Pitfall Trap

A pitfall trap is used to catch small insects that walk across the top of the ground.

YOU WILL NEED
small trowel
small plastic collecting pot
4 stones
large flat stone
piece of wood or bark

small trowel

stones

collecting pot

I Dig a hole big enough for the plastic pot to sit in.

2 Put the pot in the hole and make sure the top is level with the ground. Fill in any holes around the edge.

3 Put four stones around the top.

4 Place a large flat stone and a piece of wood over the top so that it rests on the four smaller stones. Leave overnight. Next morning look to see if any bugs or other creatures have fallen into the trap.

NATURE TIP
Don't forget to release the insects after you have studied them.

Autumn Harvest

Every year the autumn brings a rich harvest of fruit, vegetables, nuts and berries. This provides food for animals before the long winter months ahead. See if you can collect the types listed on this page.

YOU WILL NEED
basket or plastic bags
collecting pot
scissors, for snipping specimens

scissors

collecting pot

plastic bags

1 Berries that grow in hedges such as these elderberries and blackberries, have been used for centuries to make jams, fruit desserts and country wines.

2 There are different types of fruit. These fleshy fruits encourage animals to eat them and spread the seeds.

3 Nuts have a hard case to protect the seed within.

4 Seeds are produced in large numbers. They are also eaten by animals and birds.

5 These fruits are spread in the wind. Each has a tiny parachute of fine hairs or fluffy down.

6 Some fruits have hooks on them so that they catch onto animals' fur and our clothes. They can be carried for miles before they drop off and grow into a new plant.

Autumn Leaves

Every autumn deciduous trees lose their leaves. A tiny layer of cells grow across each leaf stalk like a wall, and the leaf shrivels, dies and falls off. As the leaf dies, it changes colour to yellow, brown, orange, red or purple. Collect fallen leaves and make a collage with them.

YOU WILL NEED
autumn leaves
newspaper
book
large envelope
PVA (white) glue
card (cardboard) or paper

newspaper

book

PVA (white) glue

large envelope

card (cardboard)

autumn leaves

1 Collect as many different autumn leaves as you can.

2 Place the leaves between the folds of a newspaper. Lightly press them by putting a book on top.

3 You can store the flat leaves in an envelope until you need them.

4 Glue the leaves onto a piece of card (cardboard).

5 Make a collection of different types of leaf or use them to make a collage, picture or to decorate greetings cards.

Make Your Own Museum

As time goes by you will soon build up a large collection of natural bits and pieces.

Find somewhere safe to keep your collection of specimens, notes and pictures. You could store them in a box or a cupboard. If you can find a table that is not being used, you can create your own museum with a beautiful display as shown.

Specimens look good in clear plastic boxes or stuck onto card (cardboard). You can use double-sided sticky tape or strong PVA (white) glue to stick down feathers and other treasures that you find.

Look closely at the picture opposite. Many of the things that you can see have been made using the instructions in this book. Open the pages and start to collect objects for your own museum or nature table.

Magic Compost

No garden should be without a compost bin. It is a great way to recycle food scraps and turn them into wonderful food for the soil. A few leaves are all right mixed in the compost bin, but in autumn (fall) it is better to collect and compost leaves separately because they take much longer to rot down, normally about 2 years.

YES! – Things to put in
All uncooked vegetable peelings; tea bags; banana and orange skins; apple cores; short-lived weeds; and grass cuttings (never make a thick layer, but mix these in with other things).

NO! – Things to leave out
Any cooked food; tough weeds like dandelions, clover and bindweed; evergreen leaves; sticks; and tough stems.

YOU WILL NEED
wire or plastic netting 1.5 m (5 ft) long
string
4 bamboo canes
newspaper
scissors
card (cardboard)
plastic bag

scissors

string

bamboo canes

plastic netting

newspaper

plastic bag

card (cardboard)

❗ SAFETY NOTE
Always take great care when using any sharp objects.

DID YOU KNOW?
A bin filled in spring will have rotted down and be ready to use by the end of summer, but a winter one will take longer.

1 Tie a piece of wire or plastic netting together with string to make a cylinder.

2 Thread at least 4 bamboo canes, evenly spaced through the netting. The canes should be at least 20 cm (8 in) longer than the height of the cylinder. Tie the canes to the net with string.

3 Stick the canes into the ground so they anchor the netting securely.

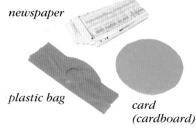

4 Line the bin well with plenty of sheets of old newspaper.

5 Start to fill with things like vegetable peelings, old tea bags and banana skins. Chop up garden clippings and put them in too.

6 Make a lid out of a piece of card (cardboard) and stick into a plastic bag to keep the rain out. When the bin is full leave it to rot down before you use it.

Spring into Action

On misty, autumn (fall) days spring might seem a long time away, but gardeners have to think ahead. If you want a cheerful pot of flowers to greet you early next year, now is the time to get planting. There are hundreds of different types of spring flowering bulbs to choose from, and mixed and matched with forget-me-nots, daisies, pansies or wallflowers, you cannot go wrong. You might wonder how the tulips will find a gap among the other plants to grow, but they will find a way to push up their strong, sturdy stems.

YOU WILL NEED
large flower pot
small stones for drainage
potting compost (soil)
tulip bulbs
wallflowers
forget-me-nots, daisies or pansies

flower pot

forget-me-nots

wallflowers

stones

potting compost (soil)

tulip bulbs

1 Use the biggest pot that you have got and put a few stones over the hole in the bottom to stop the potting compost (soil) falling out.

2 Fill the pot two-thirds full with potting compost (soil).

3 Plant about 5 tulip bulbs, making sure they are the right way up with the pointed end on top.

4 Cover the bulbs over with handfuls of potting compost (soil).

5 Using your hands to make holes, plant 3 wallflowers evenly spaced out. If you dig up a tulip bulb by mistake, just pop it back in again.

6 Fill in any gaps with forget-me-nots, double daisies or pansies, or a mixture. Give all the plants a good watering.

GARDENER'S TIP
They will not need watering a lot over the autumn (fall) and winter but they will need some, so keep an eye on the pot and if it dries out, give it a good drink.

Less Makes More

Plants that die down every winter but pop up again each spring are called border perennials. They can be expensive, but as they are often sold in quite large pots, it is possible to split them up into pieces and get perhaps three plants for the price of one.

This border perennial is called Pearl Everlasting. It has leaves which are covered with white hairs giving it a silvery appearance, and clusters of small starry flowers. The flower heads can be cut and dried – they keep perfectly.

YOU WILL NEED
good-sized pot of Pearl Everlasting
2 hand forks
trowel

Pearl Everlasting

hand forks

1 Take the plant out of its pot and push two hand forks into the plant back to back, one in the middle and the other nearer the edge.

2 Pull them apart very carefully, gently splitting the plant into two pieces, one larger than the other.

3 Split the larger piece again and take off any damaged roots and loosen some of the others.

4 Plant each piece in a flower bed about 30 cm (12 in) apart. Water in thoroughly.

GARDENER'S TIP
You can also use this method for plants like Michaelmas daisies, marsh marigolds, bleeding hearts, day-lilies and lupins (lupines) among others.

Playing Conkers

Conkers is an old game played in autumn (fall) by children throughout the British Isles. It is named after William the Conquerer.

YOU WILL NEED
horse chestnuts, or sweet chestnuts if not available
skewer
string

skewer

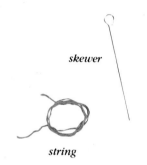

string

horse chestnuts

1 Collect horse chestnuts that have fallen on the ground. Remove the nut from its case.

!2 Ask an adult to help you drill a hole in the middle of the nut with a skewer.

3 Thread the string through the hole and tie a large knot in one end.

4 To play: The first player holds out their conker at arm's length. The second player hits the conker with theirs. Then you play in reverse. Repeat, taking turns, until one conker is broken.

!SAFETY TIP
Take care with this game! Do not eat horse chestnuts; they are mildly poisonous.

Making a Grass Squawker

This is a very simple reed instrument, but it is not very musical! It is a fun activity when out on a country walk.

YOU WILL NEED
blades of fresh grass
your hands

fresh grass

1 Look for some clean fresh grass. Carefully select and pick a long, wide blade of grass.

2 Put the blade of grass over one thumb, holding it in place with your forefinger.

NATURE TIP

Try different lengths and thicknesses of grass. Do they sound the same? If you make the hole between your thumbs bigger, does the sound change?

4 Blow through the little hole in between your two thumbs. It makes a horrible squawking noise! Replace the blade of grass if it splits.

3 Put your other thumb over the top so that the grass is held between them.

Glass Gardening

Welcome to the world of glass gardens, plants that live within a jar. This is a mini tropical rainforest, it does not need much watering because the water is recycled. Jars and bowls of almost all shapes and sizes can be transformed into a glass garden, so see what you can find. A large sweet (candy) jar does a first class job but I bet you don't get a chance to empty one of those very often!

YOU WILL NEED
gravel
glass bowl
charcoal
potting compost (soil)
selection of small houseplants
spoon and fork attached to
 pieces of cane to make
 long-handled tools for planting
plate for lid

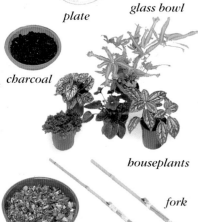

potting compost (soil)

plate

glass bowl

charcoal

houseplants

fork

gravel

spoon

1 Put a generous layer of gravel in the bottom of the container.

2 Mix two handfuls of charcoal into the potting compost (soil), then fill the container one-third full.

3 Start to plant delicate plants that are normally quite difficult to grow indoors. This is a silver fern.

4 Then add an aluminium plant and a small African violet.

5 A polka-dot plant and some creeping moss completes the planting. Now give it a thoroughly good drink to start the water cycle off.

6 Put a plate or lid on top to close the glass garden.

GARDENER'S TIP

By moving the top on and off, you can control the atmosphere inside. If water is running continuously down the sides, it is probably too wet, so take off the lid for a few days to let it dry out. Slight fogging collecting on the glass means the conditions are perfect – if there is no fogging, the conditions could be too dry and you will need to do some hand watering.

DID YOU KNOW?

Water in a glass jar is recycled in much the same way as it is in the earth's atmosphere. Inside the jar water evaporates from the surface of the soil and from the plants themselves, but rather than rising to form high clouds in the atmosphere, it collects on the inside of the glass and runs down the sides (like rain), and as the plants are watered the cycle is complete.

Monkey Nuts

Most of us like eating peanuts, but it is surprising how little most people know about the plant that they come from. In fact peanuts are not really nuts at all, but are related to peas and beans. The plant is quite small and lives for just one season. Its flowers bend down to the ground after they have been pollinated, and plant themselves in the soil where the fruit or "nuts" develop.

YOU WILL NEED
large flower pot – at least 12 cm (5 in) in diameter
potting compost (soil)
peanuts in their shells (unsalted)
cling film (plastic wrap)

potting compost (soil)

peanuts

flower pot

cling film (plastic wrap)

1 Fill a large pot with potting compost (soil) and press down lightly to make the surface level. Crack the peanuts across the middle with your fingers.

2 Plant the peanuts on their sides, putting in about 7-8 spaced evenly apart.

3 Cover them with about 2 cm (³/₄ in) of potting compost (soil) and water them well.

4 Cover the whole pot with cling film (plastic wrap) to keep them warm and moist and encourage them to grow. Remove the cling film (plastic wrap) when they have germinated, which should take about 2 weeks.

GARDENER'S TIP
Peanuts which have been roasted will not grow. Peanut plants will only produce fruit in very hot countries.

Some Pippy Ones

What is your favourite fruit – a juicy orange, a crunchy apple or perhaps a tangy lemon to make fresh lemonade? The good news is that all these fruits have pips (seeds), which could grow into plants. So instead of putting them into the dustbin (trash can), try planting them. You could grow interesting houseplants that will cost you nothing but pips (seeds) and patience.

YOU WILL NEED
orange and lemon pips (seeds)
small flower pot
potting compost (soil)

orange   *lemon*

flower pot

1 Save all the pips (seeds) you can when you are eating fruit.

2 Fill a small flower pot with potting compost (soil) and press down lightly to make the surface level. Plant the pips (seeds) by spacing them out evenly and pressing them into the compost (soil).

3 Then cover them over with about 1 cm (½ in) of potting compost (soil).

4 Water them well. Put on a sunny windowsill.

GARDENER'S TIP
When they germinate move them into individual pots. Some seeds (pips) may take up to a month to germinate.

Pineapple Plant

Pineapple tops will grow into handsome, spiky houseplants. Pineapples come from the tropics where they fruit easily, with just one pineapple growing out of the centre of each plant. There are reports of magnificent pineapple fruits being grown in English greenhouses 150 years ago, so you never know your luck!

1 Cut the topknot off with about 2 cm (³/₄ in) of flesh and leave it on its side to dry for 48 hours.

YOU WILL NEED
pineapple
knife
pebbles
flower pot about 10 cm (4 in) across the top
sand
potting soil
plastic bag
string

potting compost (soil)

string

pineapple

pineapple pebbles

sand

flower pot

knife

plastic bag

2 Put a layer of pebbles in the bottom of the pot for drainage.

3 Mix equal quantities of sand and potting compost (soil) together to make a light, well-draining mixture.

4 Fill the pot with the potting soil and sand mixture and press level lightly.

GARDENER'S TIP

After a week or two, untie the top of the bag to let in a bit of air. When you notice the leaves in the middle starting to grow again, it means you have successful rooting and the plastic bag can be removed. Don't forget to keep watering as the pineapple grows.

5 Put the pineapple top in position and cover over the fleshy part with the potting compost (soil).

6 Water in well and put the whole pot into a plastic bag tied at the top, to keep the air warm and moist, and put it on a warm windowsill.

! SAFETY NOTE

Always take great care when using any sharp objects.

Growing Exotic Plants from Seed

Other exotic plants can be grown from the seeds and pips that we find inside fruit.

YOU WILL NEED
fresh fruit
sieve
knife
paper towel
flowerpot
potting soil
plastic bag

paper towel

knife

flowerpot

plastic bag

potting soil

sieve

fresh fruit

! **1** Eat the fruit but save the seeds. Wash the seeds in the sieve. Ask an adult to help you to remove any flesh with a sharp knife. Dry the seeds on a piece of paper towel.

2 Fill the flowerpot with potting soil. Plant the seeds in the soil. Cover them with more potting soil.

3 Water, and put the flowerpot in a plastic bag. Keep in a warm place. Some seeds will sprout quickly, others may take longer. Remove the bag when the sprouts first appear. Keep the flowerpot on a windowsill. Transplant into larger flowerpots as the plants grow larger. The plants in the picture above were grown from supermarket fruit. On the left is a lemon, and on the right a tree tomato.

Cress Eggs

As long as they have water, seeds will grow in many strange places. Have fun growing these cress eggs, you can eat the cress later.

YOU WILL NEED
2 eggs
small bowl
cotton wool (ball)
water
cress seeds
coloured paints
paintbrush

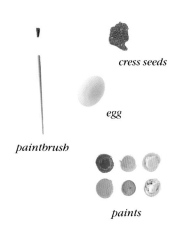

cress seeds

egg

paintbrush

paints

NATURE TIP

Look for other plants growing in unusual places such as on a roof, walls, or rocks.

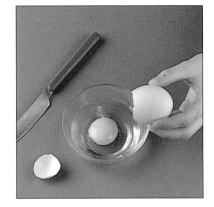

1 Carefully crack the eggs in half and empty the contents into a small bowl.

2 Moisten a piece of cotton wool (ball) in cold water and place it inside each egg shell half.

3 Sprinkle the cress seeds sparingly onto the cotton wool. Store the egg shells in a dark place for two days, or until the seeds have sprouted, then transfer to a light area such as a windowsill.

4 Paint a jolly face onto each egg shell. Give the egg a haircut and use the 'hair' as a sandwich filling.

Rhythm Sticks

Thin pieces of branch make great percussion sticks. Look out for two sticks that are about the same length and thickness next time you are in a park or wood. Make sure the branches are really dry, so that they make a loud noise when you knock them together. If you wish, seal the surface of the sticks with non-toxic craft varnish after they have been painted.

YOU WILL NEED
2 sticks
white, red, green and yellow
  poster paints
paintbrush
paint-mixing container
scissors
coloured string

scissors

string

poster paints

paintbrush

sticks

1 Remove any leaves and loose bark from the sticks and paint them white. Leave the sticks to dry.

2 Paint decorative red and green spots on top of the white paint. Make the spots different sizes.

3 When the spots have dried, fill in the white space between them with yellow paint. Leave a small white space around each dot.

4 Cut two long pieces of coloured string. Tie one to the end of each stick. Wrap the string round and round the ends of the sticks to make handles. Tie the ends of the string very tightly so that they don't unravel.

Nature Box

If you go for an autumn walk in the countryside or a park you will probably find twigs, seed pods, fir cones and so on, which make lovely decorations. This plain cardboard box has been painted green and then rows of acorns, seed pods and small and large fir cones have been added to make it really decorative. Always ask an adult to look at what you have found to see that it is safe. Carefully wash everything before you use it.

YOU WILL NEED
green poster paint
paintbrush
paint-mixing container
cardboard box, with lid
acorns, fir cones and seed pods
strong, non-toxic glue

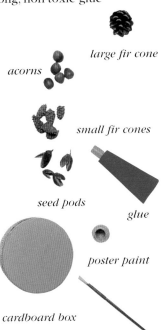

large fir cone

acorns

small fir cones

seed pods

glue

poster paint

cardboard box

paintbrush

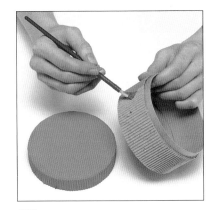

1 Paint the lid and base of the cardboard box with poster paint and leave it to dry thoroughly.

2 Arrange a row of acorns around the edge of the lid of the box and glue them in position.

3 Glue a large fir cone to the middle of the lid. Glue small fir cones to the top of the lid, between the acorns and the large fir cone.

4 Glue a row of seed pods at equal distances around the sides of the box. Let the glue dry thoroughly before you use your box.

Nature Frame

This woody frame is made out of corrugated cardboard and covered with twigs and scraps of tree bark collected on a country walk. The frame has a "spacer" in the middle, so you can push pictures into the frame from the top. You could glue fir cones on top of the twigs to make the frame even more decorative.

RECYCLING TIP
You could stick other natural items round the frame, such as feathers and little pebbles.

YOU WILL NEED
ruler
pencil
corrugated cardboard
scissors
strong, non-toxic glue
short twigs and pieces of bark

corrugated cardboard

glue

scissors

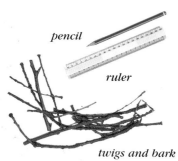

pencil

ruler

twigs and bark

1 Measure out the frame pieces on corrugated cardboard, following the pattern at the front of the book. Cut out the pieces.

2 Glue the spacer to the frame back. Make sure that the edges of the cardboard line up neatly.

3 Glue the front sections to the spacer to complete the frame.

4 Glue the twigs and pieces of bark around the frame. Choose each piece of wood carefully, so that it naturally follows the shape of the frame. Add more than one layer of twigs for greater effect.

5 Cut out a stand for the frame on a piece of cardboard.

6 Make a fold in the long side of the stand. Spread a little glue along the fold and stick the stand to the centre of the back of the frame. Allow to dry before you use your frame.

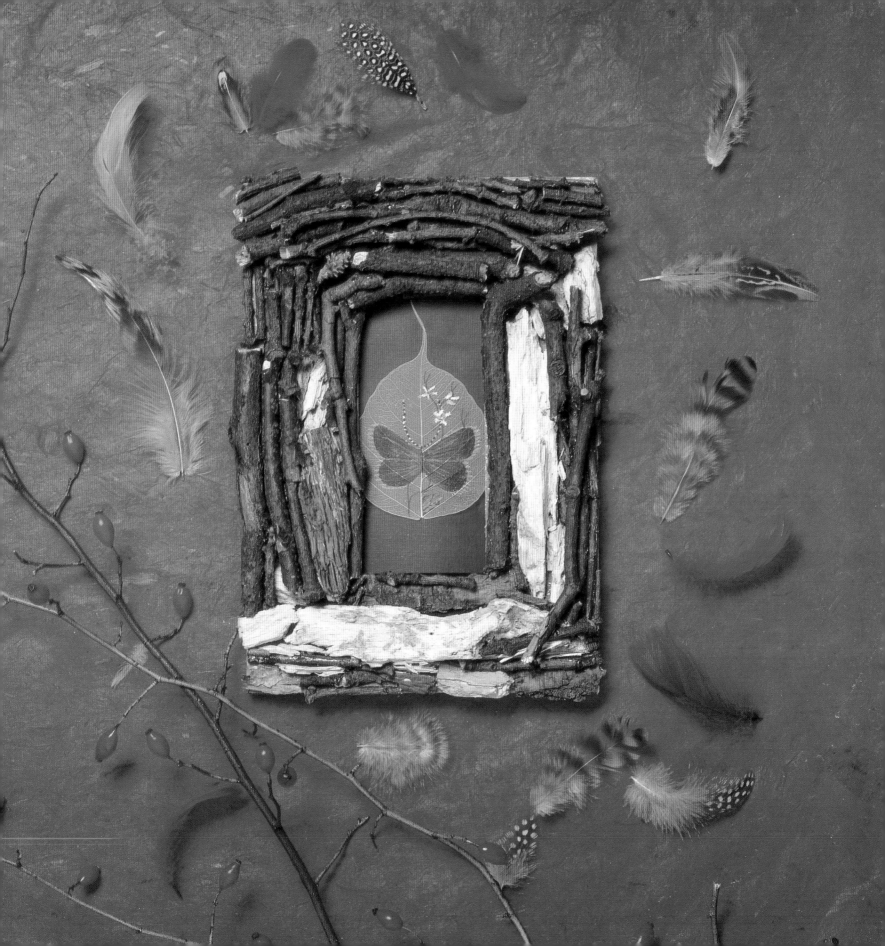

Leafy Jewellery

Use leaves and other natural 'textures' to give pattern and shape to some stunning jewellery. These pieces are very easy to make and are great gifts for your family and friends.

YOU WILL NEED
home oven-bake modelling clay
leaves
blunt knife
pencil (optional)
silver or gold modelling powder
foil dish
varnish
paintbrush
PVA (white) glue
jewellery fittings

foil dish

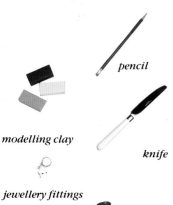

pencil

modelling clay

knife

jewellery fittings

leaves

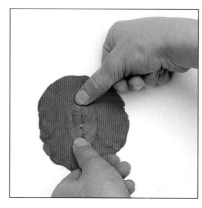

1 Soften the clay between your fingers. Keep pressing it between your fingers until you have made it into a thin sheet.

2 Place the clay on a flat surface. Press a leaf firmly down into the clay.

3 Cut the clay around the edge of the leaf with a blunt knife.

4 Lift off the leaf. Then carefully lift up the clay and twist to shape it into a natural leaf shape. Make a hole through the clay with a sharp pencil if you are making a pendant or key ring.

! 5 Dust with silver or gold modelling powder, place on a foil dish or tray, and ask an adult to help you bake the jewellery in an oven according to the clay manufacturer's instructions.

6 Varnish and stick on the jewellery fittings with glue.

Teasel Mice

In days gone by, teasels were used to comb or 'tease' tangled wool before it could be spun. You can use them to make a family of animals.

YOU WILL NEED
teasels
scissors
circle of material 23 cm (9 in) in
    diameter for the body
needle, thread and pins
soft toy stuffing
rectangle of material 23 cm × 10 cm
    (9 in × 4 in) for the arms
rectangle of material 40 cm × 10 cm
    (15 in × 4 in) for the skirt
PVA (white) glue
beads for nose and eyes
fishing line or thread for whiskers
bits and pieces of felt, string, lace
    and ribbon

teasel

soft toy stuffing

PVA (white) glue

material

lace

scissors

! 1 Collect teasels from hedges and roadsides. Cut the heads from the stalks. Be careful, they are extremely prickly. If you have trouble finding any, teasels are often sold in florists' shops for dried flower arrangements. Alternatively, you can make these mice with pine cones instead.

! 2 Sew a running stitch around the edge of the circle of cloth for the body. Pull the threads to gather.

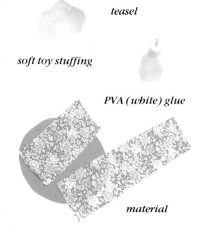

3 Put some of the toy stuffing in the middle.

4 Put a teasel on top of the stuffing. Draw the gathering thread in tightly around the base of the teasel. Knot to secure.

5 To make the arms, fold the small rectangle of material in half. Fold in half again. Pin and stitch along its length.

6 Sew a running stitch along one long side of the large rectangle of material for the skirt. Gather. Place around the neck of the teasel and stitch so that the skirt hangs over the body. Put the arms around the neck and stitch them in place above the skirt. Finish by gluing on beads for the eyes and nose, whiskers of fishing line or thread, felt ears and string for the tail. Decorate with ribbon, lace, hats, aprons, cloaks and other clothes. Make a whole family of mice!

W inter is a special time of the year: nature seems to have disappeared, but if you do some detective work in the right places you will see the tracks and trails of the tiny creatures who live there all year round. To encourage birds to visit your garden you can build a nesting box or a bird table (feeder). If you leave out their favourite foods, you will be able to watch them come and go all winter!

winter

Nature Maps

Make a map of the area around your home. You can use it to work out a nature trail. Take your friends around the trail and surprise them with all the animals and plants that you can find.

YOU WILL NEED
notebook
pencil
coloured pens

pencil

notebook

coloured pens

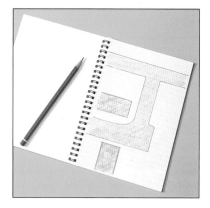

1 Draw a map of all the paths, roads, buildings and other man-made structures that you can see around your home. Colour them in grey or another suitable colour, such as brown.

2 Draw in the position of the grass, trees, hedges and other plants. Colour them in shades of green.

3 Draw in any puddles, ponds, rivers, rocks, logs, fences and any other special features that you can see.

4 On your map mark the position of any animals and plants that you find. Some may be walking around, so mark their path with a dotted line. You may only find clues, (footprints, droppings, etc) so mark these with a cross or a dot.

NATURE TIP
Use these notes and drawings to draw a large nature map of the area where you live.

154

In the Car

Car journeys can sometimes be long and boring. Help to pass the time by making a checklist in your notebook. You can check off all the natural things that you see along the way.

YOU WILL NEED
notebook
pencil
coloured pens

coloured pens

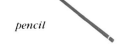

notebook

pencil

1 Make a list of the birds that you see along the way. Record how many of each you see.

2 Look for different flowers and trees on the side of the road. Look out for different colours of flowers and types of trees. Record how many of each you see.

3 Make a list of the animals you see. You can include farm animals. Record how many of each you see.

4 Make a list of the types of habitat that you pass on the way. Record how many of each you see.

Tracks and Trails

Here are some clues to look for that animals have been near, even if you have not seen them.

1 **Droppings:** This has been left by an otter. It was found on a path by a river Can you see the fish bones and water beetle wing cases? These are all that remain from the otter's meal.

NATURE TIP

You can find tracks and trails everywhere. Sometimes they are found in unusual places. Look at the picture above. Can you see the snail trail leading up and down the wall of this house?

2 **Signs of feeding:** We can often see where an animal has been eating. These feathers and rabbit bones have been left by a fox.

3 **Nests and burrows:** These show us where animals live. Can you see the muddy path leading to this burrow?

4 **Other signs:** Many animals leave scratches and other signs behind them. This fur has been caught in a fence wire.

Watching Woodlice

Woodlice cannot live in dry conditions. This experiment shows how they actively seek damp places to live.

YOU WILL NEED
collecting box
2 sheets of paper towel
shallow plastic tray
newspaper

newspaper

collecting box

shallow plastic tray

paper towel

1 Look under stones, bricks and logs for some woodlice, and put them in the collecting box.

2 Fold one piece of paper towel in half and lay it down flat in one side of the tray.

3 Fold the second piece of paper towel in half, wet it and place it in the second half of the tray.

4 Pour the woodlice onto the middle of the tray and cover with newspaper. Leave for 30 minutes. Lift up the paper. Where have the woodlice gone?

Wonderful Worms

Worms are truly wonderful creatures that we often take for granted. They keep the soil healthy by making channels for air and water and by eating plant remains. A wormery is an excellent way of making potting compost from kitchen scraps. It is on a smaller scale than a compost bin and provides a richer material which can be used for potting up plants. The type of worms that live most happily in a wormery are not earthworms which you find in the soil, but tiger worms which you can buy from most fishing tackle shops.

YOU WILL NEED
hand drill
small dustbin (trash can)
gravel
newspaper
potting compost (soil)
tiger worms
vegetable peelings

dustbin (trash can)

gravel

potting compost (soil)

vegetable peelings

tiger worms　*hand drill*　*newspaper*

1 Drill two rows of drainage holes 2.5 cm (1 in) up from the bottom of a small dustbin (trash can), plus a row of air holes around the top.

! SAFETY NOTE
Always take great care when using any type of drill.

3 Cover with a layer of wet newspaper, which stops the compost (soil) falling through onto the gravel.

2 Put a 10 cm (4-in) layer of gravel in the bottom.

4 Then add a 10 cm (4-in) layer of potting compost (soil).

5 Now add a good handful of tiger worms, use gloves if you like!

6 Add a thin layer of vegetable peelings and cover everything with a thick layer of newspaper. It will take a couple of weeks for the worms to settle into their new home. Don't add more vegetable peelings until the worms have started to work on the previous batch and only add a thin layer at a time.

DID YOU KNOW?

Worms' favourite foods are banana skins, tea-bags, carrot and potato peelings, and all greens. They are not very keen on orange or lemon skins so it is best to leave them out.

Making a Nesting Box

This box will attract small birds to nest in your garden. Once they have taken up residence, the birds will return year after year.

YOU WILL NEED
pencil
ruler
piece of wood, 147 cm × 15 cm × 1 cm (58 in × 6 in × ½ in)
saw
drill with 3 cm (1¼ in) drill bit
nails
hammer
hinge
screws
screwdriver
varnish
paintbrush

varnish

hinge

nails

hammer

drill bit

saw

ruler

pencil

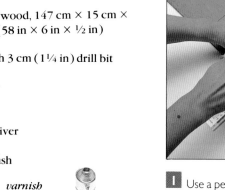

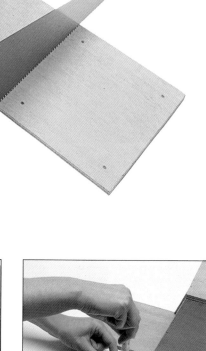

1 Use a pencil and ruler to mark out the wood. Follow the diagram opposite.

! 2 Ask an adult to help you to cut the wood.

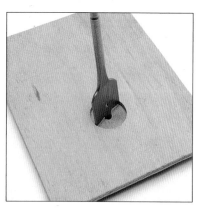

! 3 Ask an adult to drill a large hole 3 cm (1¼ in) in diameter in the front of the box. Drill four small holes in the bottom of the box and two in the back.

4 Nail the sides together and nail on the bottom of the box.

5 Screw a hinge onto the lid and attach it to the box.

6 Varnish the box and allow to dry. Place high up on a tree, post or garden shed. Attach by hammering a nail through the two holes in the back.

15 cm/6 in

bottom

top

side

side

front

back

16 cm/6½ in

22 cm/8¾ in

20 cm/8 in

24 cm/10 in

19.5 cm/7¾ in

40 cm/16 in

25 cm/10 in

20 cm/8 in

Bird Table (Feeder)

Wild birds need feeding, especially in winter time when there is little food available. Some people think you should not feed birds in spring, because chicks can choke on foods like peanuts. It is probably better not to put out any peanuts at this time of year. You will need an adult's help for this project.

YOU WILL NEED
4 strips of wood, 27 cm (10¾ in) long
square piece of wood, 30 cm × 30 cm
  (12 in × 12 in) and approximately
  1 cm (½ in) thick
nails
hammer
varnish
paintbrush
screw-eyes
string (optional)

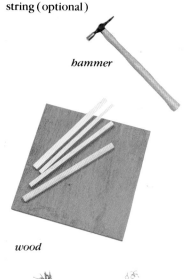

hammer

wood

nails

screw-eyes

string

1 Nail the thin strips of wood around the edges of the square piece. Leave a gap at each corner to allow the rain water to drain away.

2 Varnish and leave to dry. Screw a few screw-eyes to the underneath of the board. You can hang food from these afterwards.

3 Fix to the top of a tall post by hammering two or three nails through the middle of the board and into the post below.

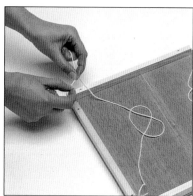

4 Alternatively, screw in one screw-eye to each corner on the upper surface. Tie on two loops of string by knotting the ends through the screw-eyes. Then you can hang the table (feeder) from a suitable tree or hook. A hanging table is best if cats are a problem in your garden.

Feeding Winter Birds

Choose some of these ideas to feed birds in winter.

YOU WILL NEED
Choose food from the following:
dried bird food
dried seed heads such as corn cobs,
   millet and sunflower
peanuts
bread and cake crumbs
coconut
lard or other hard fat
chopped bacon rind

bowl of water
peanut feeder
string
scissors
spoon
supermarket packaging such as plastic
   pots or nets

peanut feeder

lard

plastic pot

chopped rind

corn cob

dried bird food

peanuts

bread

string

1 Dried food is the easiest to put out. Give the birds grain, sunflower seeds, peanuts (but not in spring), bread and cake crumbs. Do not forget to also give them a bowl of water to drink.

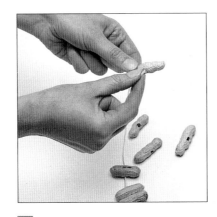

2 Hanging food allows birds to perch on the food. Hang strings of peanuts, half a coconut, a dried sweet corn cob, millet or other seed heads from the screw-eyes on your bird feeder. You can also hang these foods from the branches of nearby trees. Put loose peanuts in a peanut feeder, if feeding in the winter.

3 Birdy cake is a rich food for cold winter weather. Soften lard or a similar hard fat in a warm place. Mash in mixed grains, crumbs, bread, chopped bacon and rinds. Mix well.

4 Press into supermarket packaging such as plastic pots and nets. Set until hard in a refrigerator. When set, tip the birdy cake from the pots and put on the bird feeder or hang the nets beneath it.

Watching Animals at Night

Many animals visit our homes and gardens while we are asleep. Sometimes we are lucky enough to see them. If not, we can look for clues that they leave behind the next day.

YOU WILL NEED
torch (flashlight)
red tissue paper or cellophane
rubber band
lots of patience!

tissue paper

torch (flashlight)

rubber band

1 Cover a torch (flashlight) beam with red tissue paper or cellophane and hold it in place with a rubber band. You can shine this red light onto animals without frightening them.

2 At dusk look near trees, old buildings and lights for flying bats. Sometimes you can hear the high-pitched squeaks and clicks that they make when hunting for moths and other flying insects.

3 Look for clues such as droppings, signs of feeding, garden damage and spilt dustbins (garbage cans). (Racoons and foxes often knock these over.)

! 4 You can put food out as bait to attract wild animals and birds into your garden but you must get permission from an adult first. Try cat food, bread, grain, peanuts and peanut butter.

Making a Hide

A hide makes you invisible. You can watch animals without frightening them. Build one near a bird table and watch the birds come to feed.

YOU WILL NEED
4 long and 4 short bamboo canes
string
scissors
large dark cloth
large safety pins

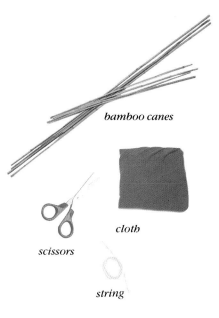

bamboo canes

cloth

scissors

string

1 Put four long canes into the ground.

2 Tie the remaining shorter canes in a square around the top.

NATURE TIP
Take a notebook and pencil into the hide so you can record what you see. Look in a field guide afterwards to identify anything you don't recognize.

3 Cover with the cloth.

4 Use safety pins to join the sides, but leave spaces big enough to look through. Remember to be very still and quiet or you will frighten away the animals you are trying to watch.

Building a Pond

Build a pond and attract more wildlife into your garden. You will be surprised just how quickly insects and other creatures will move in to use it.

YOU WILL NEED
string (optional)
spade
newspapers, old carpet, or sand
sheet of plastic or rubber pond liner
soil, logs or slabs
waterplants
fish or other creatures collected from a pond
home-grown wild flowers

spade

newspapers

sheet of plastic

1 With an adult's help, mark out the shape of the pond that you would like with string – or just mark a line in the grass. Cut the turf with a spade.

2 Dig a hole for the pond. Try to make several levels. Remove any large stones from the bottom.

3 Line the hole with newspapers, old carpet or sand.

4 Cover with a sheet of plastic or a pond liner. Carefully mould the liner to the shape of the pond. Do not stand in the pond because you will make a hole in the liner.

5 Put soil, logs or slabs over the edge of the liner. Make sure that the edge of the liner is completely covered all the way around. Fill the pond with water and leave to clear.

6 Add waterplants which are growing in pots and stand them on a brick if the water is too deep. Add fish and pond animals. Plant wildflowers that you have grown around the edge of the pond. Leave nature to do its work and in a few months you will have a mature and well established pond.

Growing Curly Beans

Here is a simple plant experiment that you can easily do at home.

YOU WILL NEED
paper towels
jam jar
bean or pea seeds such as French
(string), runner or mung beans

paper towels

jam jar

bean seeds

1 Fold a piece of paper towel in half, roll it up and put inside the jam jar.

2 Put several bean seeds between the paper and the side of the jam jar. Pour water into the bottom of the jam jar to a depth of approximately 2 cm (¾ in).

NATURE TIP
Bean shoots will always try to grow upwards and towards the light. Look at the large picture on this page. The beans top left are normal beans, growing straight up. The other two jars contain curly beans.

3 When the beans have sprouted a long shoot, turn the jam jar on its side.

4 Put the jam jar on a windowsill and turn the shoot away from the light. Keep turning the jam jar so that the shoot is turned away from the light. You will soon grow curly beans.

Colouring Celery and Flowers

This experiment works almost like magic! You can change white flowers and celery to almost any colour you like.

YOU WILL NEED
jam jar
brightly coloured water-soluble
   ink or dye
stalk of celery with leaves
white flowers such as carnations,
   chrysanthemums or daisies

water-soluble ink

celery

flowers

jam jar

1 Half-fill the jam jar with water.

2 Add some ink or dye.

!NATURE TIP

If you have difficulty making this experiment work, try again with another type or colour of dye. Remember, you will not be able to eat the celery once it has been dyed!

3 Stand some celery or flowers in the dye or ink solution.

4 You can make celery or flowers that are half one colour and half another. Split the celery or flower stalk lengthwise and put half in a jam jar of one coloured dye and the other half-stalk in the second jar containing a different colour.

Rock It

Part of the fascination of rock gardens is that it is possible to create a small piece of hillside or mountain in your own garden. Play around with the rocks until you are happy with their position and keep standing back a few paces to get a proper picture of the over all effect.

YOU WILL NEED
spade
gardening gloves
rocks
garden soil
trowel
alpine plants
grit

GARDENER'S TIP
There are many alpine plants to choose from. Most will be quite small and slow-growing which is just what you want for a rockery.

1 Wearing gardening gloves, put the biggest rock in a hole that is deep enough to bury the bottom third. Lean the rock back slightly and press in firmly.

2 Arrange the next two biggest rocks either side of the first. Fill in the gaps with some garden soil. Use lots of soil so that a mound begins to form.

3 Put two or three more rocks on the next level, making sure they are secure. Then fill in with more soil.

4 Place a final rock on the top, making sure it is still one-third buried.

5 Plant a collection of alpine plants among the rocks, putting a small handful of grit in the bottom of each planting hole – the soil on a hillside is much quicker draining than most garden soils and alpine plants don't like wet feet.

6 Cover the soil around the plants with a layer of grit, which gives it a natural finish and stops any water sitting in puddles around the plants.

Piggy-back Plant

Plants have very clever ways of making new plants. Many produce thousands of seeds each year in the hope that a few of them will land on fertile ground. The piggy-back plant, however, grows baby plantlets which it carries on its back in the middle of the leaf. If you pin these down onto a pot of potting compost (soil), they will make their own roots very quickly.

! SAFETY NOTE
Always take great care when using any sharp objects.

YOU WILL NEED
penknife
piggy-back plant
small flower pot
potting compost (soil)
small piece of wire
plastic bag
string

piggy-back plant

plastic bag

1 Using the penknife, cut off a large, healthy leaf with a plantlet in the middle.

2 Fill a small pot with potting compost (soil). Lay the leaf on top, fixing it in place by pinning it down with a U-shaped piece of wire.

string
wire

flower pot and compost

3 Water the pot thoroughly.

4 Put the pot into a plastic bag and tie the top with string.

GARDENER'S TIP
It will take 2 or 3 weeks to root. You can tell when it has rooted, because the leaves in the middle will start to grow and develop. It may need watering again during this time – if the pot feels light, water it.

Hanging Houseplants

The inch plants (Tradescantia or Wandering Jew) are perhaps the most popular of all hanging plants, being very easy to look after and happy-go-lucky. There are many different types, all with slightly different leaf colours but one thing they all share is that they are very easy to grow from cuttings – they will even root in a glass of water.

YOU WILL NEED
penknife
inch plant
glass of water
small flower pot
potting compost (soil)

⚠ SAFETY NOTE
Always take great care when using any sharp objects.

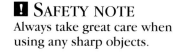

1 Using a penknife, cut off one of the tips of the plant about 5 cm (2 in) long.

2 Remove some of the lower leaves, leaving 3 or 4 at the top.

3 Put the cutting into a glass of water and put on a warm (but not too sunny) windowsill.

4 After a couple of weeks some white roots will have grown. Move the cutting to its own little pot of potting compost (soil). When it has grown another 5 cm (2 in) nip off the very tip of it. This is called pinching out and helps the plant to grow bushy instead of spindly.

Name It

Every time you sow some seeds, don't forget to stick a label in the pot. Many flowers look the same as seedlings, so if you don't label them, you could end up with monster sunflowers in a window box!

YOU WILL NEED
large plastic yoghurt pot
scissors
ruler
ballpoint pen

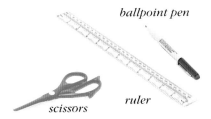

yoghurt pot

ballpoint pen

ruler

scissors

1 Cut lengthways down the side of a large yoghurt pot, then carefully cut out the bottom.

2 Open the side out flat and cut off the rim. Using a ruler and ballpoint pen, draw lines about 2 cm (³/₄ in) apart.

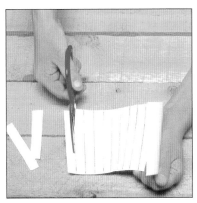
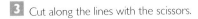

3 Cut along the lines with the scissors.

4 Cut a tapered point at one end to stick into the pot or soil. Now your labels are ready to write on.

! **SAFETY NOTE**
Always take great care when using any sharp objects.

Crazy Grass-head

Crazy grass-heads make great mates to have lounging around on your windowsill. Grow a head of long, wild green hair for a cool dude, or keep it trimmed regularly and looking neat and tidy. They cost practically nothing to make and are very original presents for your friends, if you can bear to give them away.

GARDENER'S TIP
The bottom of the sock sucks up water from the paper cup. Never let it go thirsty or the hair will wilt! Keep it on a windowsill that gets plenty of daylight.

YOU WILL NEED
old sock or pair of tights (panty hose)
scissors
grass seed
potting compost (soil)
cotton thread
elastic band
pieces of felt
fabric glue
paper cup

1 Cut off the foot of a thin, old sock or a pair of thickish tights (panty hose), with about 10 cm (4 in) of the leg.

sock

scissors *felt*

string

grass seed

cotton thread

fabric glue

paper cup *potting compost (soil)*

2 Put a generous handful of grass seed in the end of the toe and press it down in a thick layer.

! SAFETY NOTE
Always take great care when using any sharp objects.

3 Fill up the toe with potting compost (soil) pressing down each handful firmly, so you end up with a good-sized head that is quite solid. It can be any size you want but the bigger the better.

4 Knot the end like a balloon, or tie it firmly with string or strong cotton thread. Make the nose by pulling out a wodge in the middle and fixing an elastic band around the bottom.

5 Cut out the eyes, mouth and even a beard or moustache from the felt. Stick them in place using fabric glue. Leave to dry overnight. Next morning sit the head on top of a paper cup filled with water.

Making a Terrarium

Ferns grow in damp places among rocks and in woodlands. You can make yourself an indoor garden by growing them in a large jar or bottle.

YOU WILL NEED
gravel
large plastic jar or bottle with lid or
    stopper
charcoal
potting soil
spoon taped to a long stick
ferns and other plants

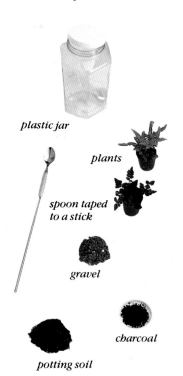

plastic jar

plants

*spoon taped
to a stick*

gravel

charcoal

potting soil

1 Put a layer of gravel in the bottom of the jar or bottle.

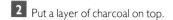

2 Put a layer of charcoal on top.

3 Put in a layer of potting soil. Smooth and level the soil with the long-handled spoon.

4 Again using the long-handled spoon, plant the ferns and other plants.

5 Gently add enough water to moisten the soil.

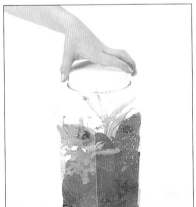

6 Replace the lid or stopper on the jar or bottle. The moisture is kept inside the jar so the plants rarely need watering.

Making a Freshwater Aquarium

Pond animals can be kept easily in an aquarium. Watch the busy lives of your pond animals.

YOU WILL NEED
aquarium gravel
bucket
large tank
newspaper
waterplants
stones or rocks
seashells (optional)
fish or other creatures collected from a pond or river

rock

aquarium gravel

newspaper

tank

1 Wash the gravel in a bucket. Keep stirring it under running water. You must do this thoroughly to remove dirt from the stones which will make the water in your tank cloudy.

2 Put the gravel in the bottom of the tank. Once you have filled the tank with water it will be too heavy to move – so decide where you want to keep it now. Do not place the tank in bright sunshine or the water will get too hot and your animals will die.

3 Put the newspaper over the top of the gravel. Slowly pour the water on to of the paper. This prevents the water from becoming too cloudy.

4 The water will be slightly cloudy, so leave the tank to clear for several days.

5 Add some waterplants and the rocks. Put the roots of the plants under the rocks to stop them from floating up to the surface. If you use any seashells, make sure that they have been well washed in fresh water to remove any salt that they may contain.

6 Put in the animals that you have collected from a pond or river. If you are going to have fish in the aquarium, only choose small ones or else they will eat all of your pond animals.

Potty over Plants

Painted pots are cheap, fun to make and very, very useful. They are also the perfect way to show off your gardening triumphs. I have used clay pots which are quite classy but plastic, or even tin, would work well too.

! SAFETY NOTE
Always take great care when using any sharp objects.

YOU WILL NEED
small clay flower pot
white primer paint and ceramic paints
paintbrush
pens
scissors
thick paper for stencils
scouring sponge

scouring sponge

thick paper

pen

scissors

ceramic paints

flower pot

white primer paint

paintbrush

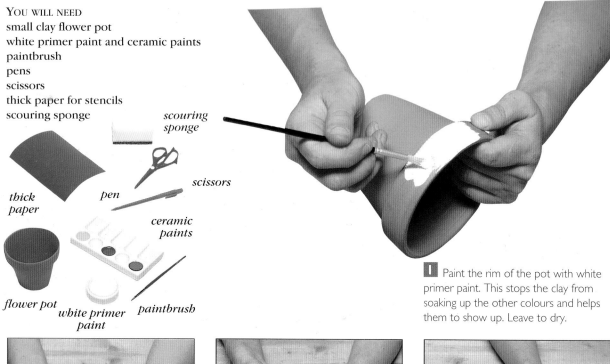

1 Paint the rim of the pot with white primer paint. This stops the clay from soaking up the other colours and helps them to show up. Leave to dry.

2 Draw simple leaf and petal patterns on a piece of paper.

3 Cut the patterns out carefully to make stencils.

4 Cut a scouring sponge into small pieces with the scissors.

5 Place the stencil on the pot rim. Dip the corners of the sponge pieces into the ceramic paints and dab lightly on the cut-out pattern. Lift the paper off carefully and work around the pot.

6 Finish the details, like flower centres or stalks with a paintbrush.

Pine Cone Mobile

Pine cones are lovely objects and they look great suspended from a mobile. The bars of this mobile are made from lengths of twig and the pine cones are tied at different heights. Pine cones are very much a part of winter, and you could paint your twigs and cones with gold or silver poster paint to make a Christmas mobile.

YOU WILL NEED
scissors
thin coloured cord
pine cones
2 thin twigs and 1 forked twig

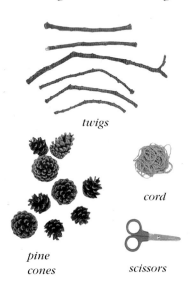

twigs

cord

pine cones

scissors

1 Cut lengths of cord and attach each one to the top of a cone. Tie a cone to both ends of two short twigs.

2 Tie the two twigs together with the cord, one above the other, to make the mobile shape.

3 Tie more small pine cones to the lower section of the mobile. Hang them at different heights.

4 Tie a large forked twig to the upper twig. Wrap the two together tightly by winding cord around them. Tie a length of cord to the top of the mobile to make a hanger.

Herby Vinegar

What a difference a sprig or two of herbs makes to a bottle of boring old vinegar! It looks much prettier and the hint of herbs gives it a more interesting flavour. It makes a great gift too.

YOU WILL NEED
sprigs of assorted herbs
pretty glass bottle with a cork top
cider or wine vinegar
label and pen

glass bottle with a cork top

label

pen

vinegar

herbs

1 Pick some herbs from the garden, look for perfect leaves without any marks or insect bites. Good herbs are rosemary, purple sage, thyme and marjoram.

2 Trim, wash and dry the herbs and put a selection of them in the bottle.

DID YOU KNOW?
Use your herb vinegar within two weeks, otherwise it will become poisonous.

3 Fill the bottle with cider or white wine vinegar. Put the top on securely.

4 Label the bottle. You can start to use the vinegar straight away.

Hyacinths for Winter

Every year I have a competition with myself to try to get bowls of sweetly scented hyacinths in flower for Christmas. The secret is to plant them as soon as you see the bulbs for sale in garden centres at the end of the summer. Buy the largest bulbs you can and choose those that are described as "prepared". This means that they have been tricked by the grower into thinking that it is spring and time for them to wake up and start growing.

YOU WILL NEED
pretty pot
pebbles
potting compost (soil)
hyacinth bulb
newspaper

potting compost (soil)

pot

pebbles

hyacinth bulb

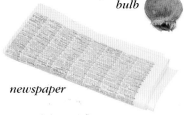

newspaper

1 Fill a pretty pot, or decorate one yourself and put a few pebbles in the bottom for drainage.

2 Fill the pot half-full with potting compost (soil).

3 Plant the hyacinth bulb, putting some compost around it but leaving the top of the bulb, which is called the nose, just showing. Water the pot well.

4 Cover the pot with a thick layer of newspaper to keep out the light. Put it somewhere cool like a shed or unheated room for 6 weeks. During this time water once or twice. After 6 weeks, take off the newspaper, put the pot on a windowsill, and wait for the flowers to come.

Happy Christmas Tree

If you buy a Christmas tree with roots on and look after it properly, it can last for years. The tree in the photograph is 5 years old and still going strong! The most important thing is not to let it get too hot and dry because it would really rather be outside in the winter snow and ice than in your cozy living room.

YOU WILL NEED
Christmas tree with roots on
a large pot
potting compost (soil)
plate for pot to stand on
watering can
Christmas decorations

Christmas tree

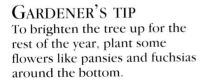

large pot   *potting compost (soil)*   *watering can*

1 As soon as you buy the tree, move it into a larger pot so there is at least a 2 cm (³/₄ in) gap between the roots and the sides of the pot. Fill the gap with compost (soil) and press down firmly.

GARDENER'S TIP
To brighten the tree up for the rest of the year, plant some flowers like pansies and fuchsias around the bottom.

2 Put the tree in a position where you can enjoy looking at it, but where it is cool, well away from fires or radiators. Find a large plate for the pot to stand in and give the tree a good drink of water.

3 Choose Christmas decorations which fit the size of the tree.

4 When Christmas is over, put the tree in its pot back outside as soon as possible, in a sheltered corner away from any strong winds.

Natural Christmas Decorations

In ancient times people in Europe worshipped many different gods of nature. Holly, ivy, mistletoe, yew and other plants held religious meaning for these people. Memories have been passed down with our folklore. Today, these plants are still used to decorate homes at Christmas.

YOU WILL NEED
Christmas greenery
newspaper
dried seed heads
pine cones
gold and silver spray paint
florist's foam for flower arranging
candles
red berries
Christmas tree decorations
ribbon
sticky tape
string
wire
tinsel

spray paint

candle

florist's foam

string

tinsel

1 Gather together some greenery such as holly, ivy, mistletoe, conifer sprigs and other evergreen leaves.

2 Spread out the newspaper in a well ventilated area. Spray dried seed heads and pine cones with gold or silver paint. Allow to dry before using as decorations.

3 To make a table decoration, stick greenery into florists' foam.

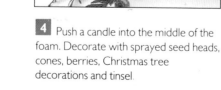

4 Push a candle into the middle of the foam. Decorate with sprayed seed heads, cones, berries, Christmas tree decorations and tinsel.

5 To make a Christmas wreath, tape or tie greenery around a circle of wire, cane or twigs.

6 Decorate with pine cones and ribbons and other pretty objects. Look at the picture opposite. Can you see some other ideas for natural Christmas decorations?

Useful Addresses

Many of the organizations below offer junior membership, and information and activities on environmental issues. Others maintain reserves open to visitors.

UNITED KINGDOM

British Trust for Conservation Volunteers
36 St Mary's Street
Wallingford
Oxon OX10 0EU
Tel: (01865) 810 215
Information on practical conservation work.

Countryside and Wildlife Branch
The Environment Service
Calvert House
35 Castle Street
Belfast
BT1 1GU
Tel: (01232) 314 911

Country Naturalist's Trust
Consult your local library for information.

English Nature
Northminster House
Northminster Road
Peterborough
Northants PE1 1EU
Tel: (01733) 349 345

Friends of the Earth
26–28 Underwood Street
London N1 7JO
Tel: (0171) 490 1555

Greenpeace
Canonbury Villas
London N1 2PN
Tel: (0171) 354 5100

Royal Society for Nature Conservation
The Green
Witham Park
Waterside South
Lincolnshire IN5 7JR
Tel: (01522) 544 400

Royal Society for the Protection of Birds
The Lodge
Sandy
Bedfordshire SG19 2DL
Tel: (01767) 680 551

Royal Society for the Prevention of Cruelty to Animals
The Manor House
Causeway
Sussex RH12 1HG
Tel: (01403) 264 181

Worldwide Fund for Nature
Panda House
Weyside Park
Surrey GU7 1XR
Tel: (01483) 426 444

UNITED STATES

American Horticultural Society
7931 East Boulevard Drive
Alexandria
VA 22308
Tel: (703) 768 5700

Friends of the Earth
218 D. Street, S.E.
Washington
DC 20003
Tel: (202) 783 7400

Friends of the Everglades
101 Westward Drive, 2
Miami Springs
FL 33166
Tel: (305) 888 1230

Greenpeace USA
1436 U. St., N.W.
Washington
DC 20009
Tel: (202) 462 1177

International Wildlife Conservation
c/o NY Zoological Society
Bronx
NY 10460
Tel: (718) 220 5100

Kids for a Clean Environment
P.O. Box 188254
Nashville
TN 37215
Tel: (615) 331 7381

Rainforest Action Network
450 Sansome Street, 700
San Francisco
CA 94111
Tel: (415) 398 4404

World Wildlife Fund
1250 24th Street, N.W.
Washington
DC 20037
Tel: (1202) 293 4800

AUSTRALIA

Melbourne Zoo Education Service
Elliot Avenue
Victoria 305
Tel: (03) 285 9300

National Parks and Wildlife
See the district office in your local telephone directory.

Royal Society for the Prevention of Cruelty to Animals
See your local telephone directory.

Taronga Zoo Education Centre
Mosman
New South Wales 2088
Tel: (02) 969 2455

Western Plains Zoo
Education Department
Dubbo
Tel: (068) 825 888

Index